REALM OF
THE IROQUOIS
✢

TIME®
LIFE
BOOKS

Other Publications:

WEIGHT WATCHERS₈ SMART CHOICE RECIPE COLLECTION
TRUE CRIME
THE ART OF WOODWORKING
LOST CIVILIZATIONS
ECHOES OF GLORY
THE NEW FACE OF WAR
HOW THINGS WORK
WINGS OF WAR
CREATIVE EVERYDAY COOKING
COLLECTOR'S LIBRARY OF THE UNKNOWN
CLASSICS OF WORLD WAR II
TIME-LIFE LIBRARY OF CURIOUS AND UNUSUAL FACTS
AMERICAN COUNTRY
VOYAGE THROUGH THE UNIVERSE
THE THIRD REICH
THE TIME-LIFE GARDENER'S GUIDE
MYSTERIES OF THE UNKNOWN
TIME FRAME
FIX IT YOURSELF
FITNESS, HEALTH & NUTRITION
SUCCESSFUL PARENTING
HEALTHY HOME COOKING
UNDERSTANDING COMPUTERS
LIBRARY OF NATIONS
THE ENCHANTED WORLD
THE KODAK LIBRARY OF CREATIVE PHOTOGRAPHY
GREAT MEALS IN MINUTES
THE CIVIL WAR
PLANET EARTH
COLLECTOR'S LIBRARY OF THE CIVIL WAR
THE EPIC OF FLIGHT
THE GOOD COOK
WORLD WAR II
HOME REPAIR AND IMPROVEMENT
THE OLD WEST

*For information on and a full description of any of the
Time-Life Books series listed above, please call
1-800-621-7026 or write:*
Reader Information
Time-Life Customer Service
P.O. Box C-32068
Richmond, Virginia 23261-2068

This volume is one of a series that chronicles the history and culture of the Native Americans. Other books in the series include:

THE FIRST AMERICANS
THE SPIRIT WORLD
THE EUROPEAN CHALLENGE
PEOPLE OF THE DESERT
THE WAY OF THE WARRIOR
THE BUFFALO HUNTERS

The Cover: Carved from a single piece of wood, an Iroquois club from the mid-19th century bears the haunting image of a tattooed warrior. Although the Iroquois were renowned as fierce combatants, this finely carved weapon testifies to their skill as superb artisans.

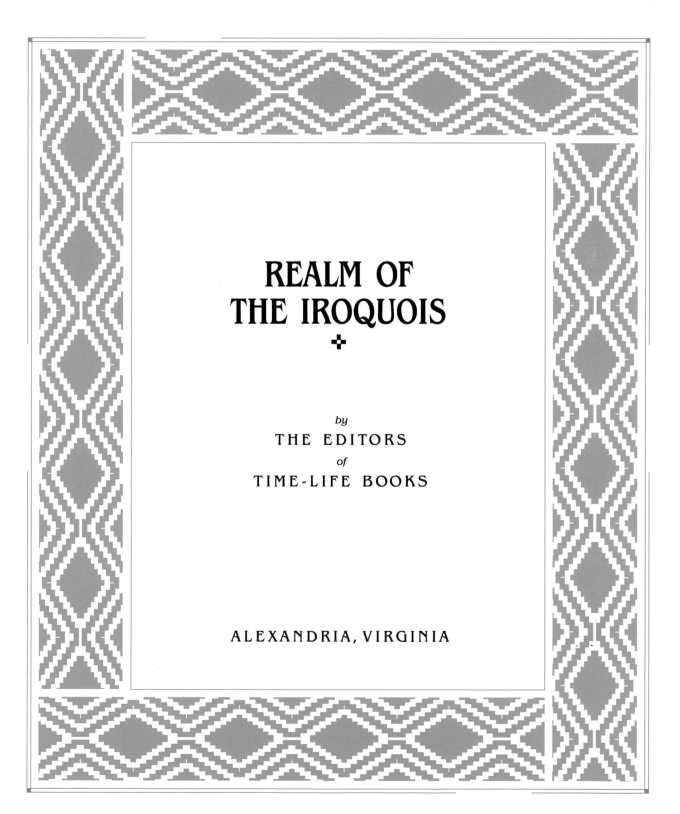

REALM OF THE IROQUOIS

✤

by
THE EDITORS
of
TIME-LIFE BOOKS

ALEXANDRIA, VIRGINIA

TIME-LIFE BOOKS

EDITOR-IN-CHIEF: Thomas H. Flaherty
Director of Editorial Resources: Norma E. Shaw (acting)
Executive Art Director: Ellen Robling
Director of Photography and Research: John Conrad Weiser
Editorial Board: Dale M. Brown, Janet Cave, Roberta Conlan, Robert Doyle, Laura Foreman, Jim Hicks, Rita Thievon Mullin, Henry Woodhead

PRESIDENT: John D. Hall

Vice President and Director of Marketing: Nancy K. Jones
Editorial Director: Russell B. Adams, Jr.
Director of Production Services: Robert N. Carr
Production Manager: Marlene Zack
Director of Technology: Eileen Bradley
Supervisor of Quality Control: James King

Editorial Operations
Production: Celia Beattie
Library: Louise D. Forstall
Computer Composition: Deborah G. Tait (Manager), Monika D. Thayer, Janet Barnes Syring, Lillian Daniels
Interactive Media Specialist: Patti H. Cass

Time-Life Books is a division of Time Life Incorporated

PRESIDENT AND CEO: John M. Fahey, Jr.

Library of Congress Cataloging in Publication Data
Realm of the Iroquois/by the editors of Time-Life Books.
     p.   cm. — (The American Indians)
     Includes bibliographical references (p.   ) and index.
     ISBN 0-8094-9437-X
     ISBN 0-8094-9438-8 (lib. bdg.)
     1. Iroquoian Indians.   2. Wyandot Indians.
     I. Time-Life Books.   II. Series.
E99.I69R43   1993   92-39727
973'.04975—dc20   CIP

THE AMERICAN INDIANS

SERIES EDITOR: Henry Woodhead
Administrative Editor: Jane Edwin

Editorial Staff for *Realm of the Iroquois*
Senior Art Directors: Dale Pollekoff (principal), Ray Ripper
Picture Editor: Jane Coughran
Text Editors: Stephen G. Hyslop (principal), John Newton
Writers: Maggie Debelius, Stephanie Lewis
Associate Editors/Research: Kirk E. Denkler, Catherine Chase Tyson (principals), Harris J. Andrews, Robert H. Wooldridge, Jr.
Assistant Art Director: Susan M. Gibas
Senior Copyeditor: Ann Lee Bruen
Picture Coordinator: David C. Beard
Editorial Assistant: Gemma Villanueva

Special Contributors: Amy Aldrich, Ronald H. Bailey, Susan Perry, Lydia Preston, David S. Thomson (text); Martha Lee Beckington, Barbara Fleming (research); Barbara L. Klein (index).

Correspondents: Elisabeth Kraemer-Singh (Bonn), Christine Hinze (London), Christina Lieberman (New York), Maria Vincenza Aloisi (Paris), Ann Natanson (Rome). Valuable assistance was also provided by: Saskia Van de Linde (Amsterdam), Corky Bastlund (Copenhagen), John Dunn (Melbourne), Elizabeth Brown (New York).

General Consultants
Frederick E. Hoxie is director of the D'Arcy McNickle Center for the History of the American Indian at the Newberry Library in Chicago. Dr. Hoxie is the author of *A Final Promise: The Campaign to Assimilate the Indians 1880-1920* and other works. He has served as a history consultant to the Cheyenne River and Standing Rock Sioux tribes, Little Big Horn College archives, and the Senate Select Committee on Indian Affairs. He is a trustee of the National Museum of the American Indian in Washington, D.C.

Dean R. Snow, Professor of Anthropology at the State University of New York at Albany, has written numerous archaeological books and articles, including *Archaeology of New England* and the *Atlas of Ancient America,* which he coauthored. Dr. Snow is a member of the Society for American Archaeology and a fellow of the American Association for the Advancement of Science. He is currently involved in the Mohawk Valley Project, a demographic archaeological study of the rise and decline of the Mohawk nation and an operation to salvage its artifacts.

Special Consultant
Richard Hill is a member of the Beaver Clan of the Tuscarora Nation of the Six Nations Reserve of Ontario, and resides at the Tuscarora Indian Reservation, Sanborn, N.Y. He is a lecturer in Native American Studies at the State University of New York at Buffalo, has curated several exhibitions on Iroquois art, culture, and history, and has written extensively on those subjects. He currently serves as Assistant Director for Public Programs for the National Museum of the American Indian.

CONTENTS

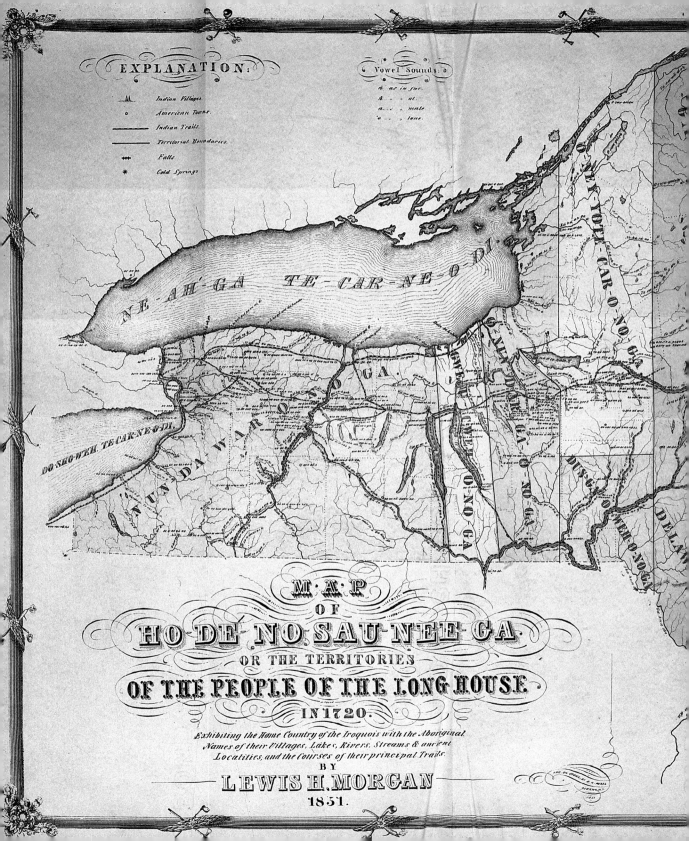

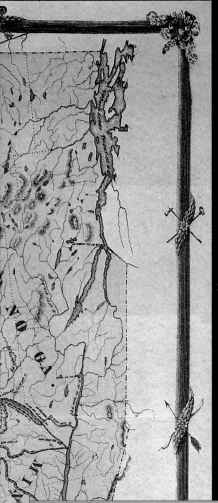

THE LAND OF IROQUOIA

The large map, based on research among the Iroquois by pioneering anthropologist Lewis H. Morgan, shows the territories of the Hodenosaunee, or "People of the Longhouse," in the year 1720. Each nation's area is identified on the map by its Iroquois name; the Iroquois Trail network is marked with a broken line. The small map (inset) provides present-day placenames.

From the banks of the Hudson River to the shores of Lake Erie, the people of the Iroquois League dwelt in a land that "possessed many advantages superior to any other part of America," according to one Iroquois. Towering forests, teeming rivers, and fertile marshes provided the inhabitants with a bounty of wild plants, game, waterfowl, and fish.

Originally five feuding tribes, the Iroquois peoples formed a confederacy by the 16th century that gave each nation claim to a portion of the abundant land. They likened their political edifice to a longhouse, their traditional dwelling place in which several families lived under one roof, with separate fires and partitions for privacy. The Mohawk guarded the eastern door of the symbolic longhouse with a domain that overlooked the Mohawk Valley. At the western door were the Seneca, with land that stretched almost as far as Niagara Falls. Between the two outlying nations burned the council fires of the Oneida, the Onondaga, and the Cayuga.

A 240-mile-long central trail, running approximately from present-day Albany to Buffalo, linked the nations of the confederacy. Conforming to the country's topography, the trail was so efficient that the current New York State Thruway traces much of its route. A network of smaller paths branched out from the central trail to connect all of Iroquoia. The photographs shown on the following pages depict this timeless landscape.

MOOSE RIVER located in the southwestern Adirondacks, at one time served as a hunting and fishing ground for the Iroquois peoples who lived east of Lake Ontario. During the 16th century, the neighboring Mohawk laid claim to the fertile territory.

SCUDDERS FALLS (inset) tumbles into Zimmerman Creek about one mile above the Mohawk River at the center of Mohawk territory. The Keepers of the Eastern Door set up their principal villages along the Mohawk River just west of the head of the Iroquois Trail.

MOOSE RIVER

SCUDDERS FALLS

SELKIRK SHORES, on the southeastern edge of Lake Ontario, is land that was once contested but eventually became home to the Oneida. The flora of the region was particularly valued by Iroquois herbalists who employed the trillium plant, whose white flowers blanket the forest floor, for treating rheumatism, headache, itches, and chapped hands.

• SELKIRK SHORES

ONEIDA LAKE

ONEIDA LAKE (above), situated northeast of present-day Syracuse, once yielded valuable harvests of salmon and other migratory fish. Such bounty sustained the Oneida, whose name means "People of the Erected Rock" or "Granite People."

CHITTENANGO FALLS >>>>>>>>>> cascading down a limestone escarpment, was within the domain of the Onondaga, or "People on the Hills."

Because they lived in the heart of Iroquois country, the Onondaga were known as the Keepers of the Central Fire in the symbolic longhouse.

CHITTENANGO FALLS ●

**TAUGHANNOCK
FALLS** ≫≫≫≫≫≫≫≫
*(inset) plummets 215
feet into the gorge
of Cayuga Lake, a*
*drop that exceeds
Niagara Falls by 55
feet. Legend has it
that the landmark
was named for*
*Taughannock, a
Delaware chief who
was thrown over the
falls by Cayuga war-
riors. A less vivid*
*explanation holds
that Taughannock
is an Iroquois word
meaning "Great
Falls in the Woods."*

MONTEZUMA MARSH

TAUGHANNOCK FALLS

MONTEZUMA MARSH >>>>>>>>>>>> at the head of Cayuga Lake, has sustained the Cayuga people for centuries with its treasure-trove of geese, ducks, swans, and other waterfowl.

THE GENESEE RIVER >>>>>>>>>>> *flows through the heart of Seneca country in a 600-foot-deep gorge. According to an Iroquois legend, one of these hills gave birth to the first members of the nation; the Seneca accordingly called themselves the Great Hill People.*

GENESEE RIVER

RED HOUSE LAKE (inset) feeds the Allegheny River in southwestern New York State. Today, one of three remaining Seneca reservations is located a few miles away.

ALABAMA SWAMPS

RED HOUSE LAKE

ALABAMA SWAMPS, important to the Seneca, lay near the western end of the old Iroquois Trail. It took Iroquois relay runners about 70 hours to carry messages the entire length of the trail.

1

FORGING AN ALLIANCE

Sky Woman, source of earthly bounty in the Iroquois tale of creation, plummets from heaven through a gap left by a tree uprooted by her angry mate, Sky Chief, in this painting by Seneca artist Ernest Smith. As Sky Woman hurtled toward the waters below, waterfowl spread their wings to cushion her fall, and she landed safely on a turtle's back, which became the foundation for the earth and for the crops that Sky Woman's progeny bequeathed to the Iroquois.

Before the Five Nations of the Iroquois came together and framed their Great League of Peace, legends attest, they knew no shelter from strife. "Everywhere there was peril and everywhere mourning," an Iroquois tale relates. "Feuds of sister towns, and feuds of families and of clans made every warrior a stealthy man who liked to kill." It was said that during this time of unremitting conflict, an Onondaga chieftain suffered a terrible blow—he lost his wife and three daughters in swift succession. Some members of the community attributed the deaths to the demonic shaman of the Onondaga Indians, Atotarho, whose evil medicine had claimed the lives of a number of people and had so infected his own being that snakes coiled menacingly around his brow.

Consumed by sorrow and rage, the bereaved chief wandered into the forest. For Iroquois mourning the loss of loved ones in those days, there seemed to be only one way to assuage grief and make restitution to the dead—to claim the life of one's enemy in return. But this sufferer, known to posterity as Hiawatha, would find a new way of appeasing his furies, and that discovery would go far toward reconciling his people. In the depths of the forest, Hiawatha came upon a lake, where ducks swam peacefully as they had on the all-enveloping waters at the beginning of time. Miraculously, the ducks lifted the water with their wings so that Hiawatha could cross in dry moccasins. On the lake bed he beheld beautiful shells and threaded them on rushes. Holding the shell strings in his hand, he said to himself: "This would I do if I found anyone burdened with grief even as I am. I would take these shell strings in my hand and console them. The strings would become words and lift away the darkness with which they are covered. Holding these in my hand, my words would be true." Thus, Hiawatha conceived the first wampum.

Still grieving, he resumed his wanderings. Every night he picked up the wampum strings and repeated the plea for condolence, hoping someone would hear; but no one came to take away his sorrow. Then one night in his agony, he was visited by an incarnation of mercy, a healing spirit in human form known as Deganawida. In later times, Iroquois who were familiar with Christian teachings would speak of Deganawida as their savior, born of a virgin and sent by the Creator to spread the good news of peace and power. In his appointed role as peacemaker, according to tradition, Deganawida soothed Hiawatha and taught him the means of allaying the passions that had set one Iroquois against another in the past. Using words that would become part of the solemn mourning rituals of the Iroquois League, Deganawida took up the wampum strings and offered Hiawatha condolence. "I wipe away the tears from your face using the white fawn skin of pity," he said. "I make it daylight for you. I beautify the sky." The gracious words lifted Hiawatha's grief, and he was able to reason once more. Subsequently, he and Deganawida set out to compose the laws of the great peace, appointing a string of wampum for each law in order to help future generations remember and recite the principles of their accord.

Carrying the wampum from one village to the next, Deganawida and Hiawatha taught the laws of peace to the Iroquois people, and soon they succeeded in persuading the chiefs of four nations—the Mohawk, the Oneida, the Cayuga, and the Seneca—to join in the Great League of Peace. The lone holdout was the venomous Onondaga shaman, Atotarho. Braving his fury, Hiawatha promised Atotarho that if he accepted

Native to the northern woodlands, a fox crouches attentively in this drawing by French missionary Louis Nicolas, who lived among the Indians of New France from 1667 to 1674.

Another Nicolas drawing portrays an Iroquois warrior in body paint attacking a burning enemy longhouse. Scalps dangle from poles at either end of the dwelling.

the good news, he would be
guardian of the council fire of all
five nations. "The smoke of that
fire shall reach the sky," he assured
Atotarho, "and be seen of all men." In
order to calm the shaman's troubled
mind, Hiawatha combed the snakes from his hair.
At last Atotarho yielded to Hiawatha's induce-
ments, and the Onondaga committed to the league.

Deganawida placed deer antlers on the heads of
the chiefs of the Five Nations to symbolize their authority. He proclaimed to all that the league would take
the form of the longhouse—the traditional home of the
Iroquois, in which many families, each with its own fire,
lived together as a single household; in the same way, the
Five Nations would from that time forward associate as
one family, with the Onondaga at the center. His work
done, Deganawida withdrew from the sight of men. "If the great peace
should fail," he said in parting, "call my name, and I will return."

Heavily tattooed on arms and legs, a young Iroquois drawn by Nicolas puffs on a pipe while holding a tomahawk with a metal head that was obtained in trade with Europeans.

Although versions of this tale were not committed to writing until the
19th century, the core of the legend harks back several hundred years to
the pivotal event in Iroquois history—the founding, not long before the
arrival of the first Europeans, of the Great League of Peace, an extraordi-
nary compact that altered the destiny of the Iroquois and all peoples who
came in contact with them. As the legend makes clear, that compact was
designed to put an end to an ancient cycle of feuding, marked by acts of
extreme cruelty. Indeed, in some versions of the founding legend, Hiawatha first appears as a cannibal who is persuaded by the peacemaker to
renounce the eating of human flesh, a treatment the Iroquois sometimes
accorded enemy prisoners during prolonged rites of torture and sacrifice.

The historic achievement of the Great League of Peace was to prevent aggrieved members of the Five Nations from committing such provocative deeds—and other forms of retribution—against their fellow Iroquois. But the compact did not lessen hostilities with outside groups. To
the contrary, it led avid young warriors to seek new enemies elsewhere

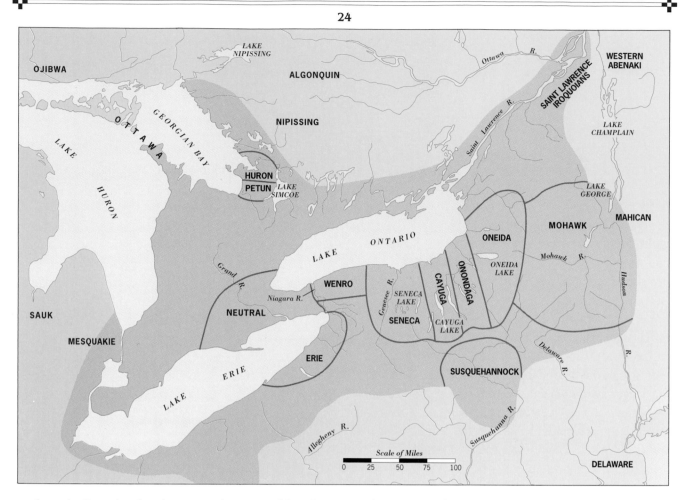

and made it easier for the Iroquois to combine forces against external foes. Thus the founders of the league bequeathed a divided legacy to future generations, one of inner harmony and outward strife. Adept at both conciliation and conflict, the Iroquois posed an unprecedented challenge not only for rival tribes but also for contending European factions in the area—the French to the north and the Dutch and later the English to the south. In the end, the twin burdens of coping with European intrusions and battling resistant tribes would prove too much for the Iroquois, and their bid for regional dominion would collapse. Yet they would persevere as a culture, guided by prophets who reinterpreted their ancestral legends and ceremonies and renewed their epic quest for peace and power.

The people of the original Five Nations, whose twin talents for war making and alliance building left a lasting impression on friends and foes alike, were just one of several branches of the Iroquoian language family, whose members shared many customs. When Europeans first reached the New World, there were perhaps as many as 100,000 Iroquoian speakers in the Northeast, inhabiting a narrow corridor of land along the Saint Lawrence River and a broad swath of territory around the eastern Great Lakes, including most of present-day New York State and the southern portions of Quebec and Ontario. The domain of these Iroquoians, as they are known collectively, was not vast, but it embraced some of the richest

By the 16th century, when Europeans first made contact, the Iroquoian speakers of the Northeast dominated large sections of the interior (shaded above). These Iroquoians comprised several independent groups— among them the Susquehannock, Petun, and Erie—and two major alliances: the Huron tribes living in close proximity near Georgian Bay and the Five Nations of the Iroquois League spread out across present-day New York State. During the 17th century, warriors of the Five Nations first devastated the rival Huron and then dispersed or incorporated all the remaining Iroquoians.

An Iroquois snow-shoe, made in the 1800s with a hickory frame and a webbing of twisted tree bark, resembles those used earlier by hunters of the region, who could cover up to 50 miles of snow-covered terrain a day wearing the devices.

planting and hunting grounds in the Northeast and offered the readiest access by trail or waterway from the Atlantic Ocean to the heart of the continent. At exactly what time the Iroquoians came to occupy this vital position remains unclear. They may have inhabited the region for a thousand years or more before whites encountered them. Or it is possible that they migrated to the Northeast as recently as AD 1000 from the southern woodlands, where a few isolated Iroquoian-speaking groups such as the Cherokee would remain. Whatever their origins, the northern Iroquoians gradually subdivided into distinct groups. By AD 1500 the region was home to approximately a dozen tribes—or nations, as they would proudly refer to themselves in their dealings with the Europeans.

Despite similarities of language and culture, these groups pursued fiercely independent existences, frequently waging war on one another or on nearby Algonquian-speaking tribes. Indeed, the word *Iroquois* derived from an uncomplimentary term that was applied to them by their Algonquian rivals, who told Basque fishermen frequenting the Northeast coast in the 16th century of fierce warriors who dominated the interior. The Basques called them Hilokoa, or the "Killer People." French traders subsequently modified the term to its present form. Thus the Iroquois, like so many other Native American groups, were branded with a title unrelated to the name they chose for themselves—the Hodenosaunee, or "People of the Longhouse."

The Hodenosaunee were not the only Iroquoian peoples to have formed an alliance by the time white men arrived. To the northwest, along Lake Huron's Georgian Bay, dwelt another league of five Iroquoian-speaking nations known collectively as the Wendat, meaning "Islanders" or "Dwellers on a Peninsula"—a reference both to the land on which they lived, which jutted out into Georgian Bay, and to their belief that they were created to inhabit the center of the great island earth. They, too, received a dismissive title from outsiders by which they later became known: Explorers from France labeled them the Huron, derived from a French word meaning "wild boar" but used loosely to signify "savage."

Men hold hands in ceremonial fashion around the border of this 18th-century Iroquois buckskin robe, made from a single large deer hide. The designs on the robe, including images of plants and animals found in the region, were meticulously embroidered with dyed porcupine quills.

The Huron alliance proved to be weaker politically and militarily than the League of Five Nations and ultimately yielded to its assertive rival. But when the French first appeared, the Huron, who numbered about 20,000, were almost as populous as the Iroquois and, for a time, even more prosperous. They welcomed the traders of New France who ventured up the Saint Lawrence and profited by early exchanges with them, unable to foresee the drastic consequences—including epidemics of European-borne diseases and an infusion of Jesuit missionaries intent on changing native ways. In their journals, the Jesuits meticulously documented Huron culture even as they altered it, providing the basis for much of what is known today about ancestral Iroquoian traditions.

Early contacts yielded less information about the other Iroquoian peoples living beyond the pale of the two major alliances. These included the Erie, who occupied the southeastern edge of that lake; the Susquehannock, or "People at the Falls," who inhabited the Susquehanna River valley in southern New York State until about 1570, when they migrated to south-central Pennsylvania; the Petun, or "Tobacco People," who raised that sacred plant along with other crops below Georgian Bay, near Huron territory; the confederated Neutral of the western shores of Lake Ontario, who earned their name because they stood apart from hostilities between the Iroquois and the Huron; and the shadowy Saint Lawrence Iroquoians, who met the first French expeditions up that river in the mid-16th century but had vanished from the scene by the time the foreigners returned a few decades later. These elusive groups were the subject of much conjecture. The English adventurer John Smith described the Susquehannock as "giant-like people," for example, although the archaeological record indicates that Susquehannock men were of average height for their time—about five feet four inches. Judging by the more reliable references to them in journals and diaries, the other Iroquoians may have lacked the clout of the populous Iroquois or Huron but shared many of their cultural characteristics.

Large or small, the various Iroquoian groups drew on a common endowment—a natural setting that demanded much from those who braved its extremes but offered surprising bounty in return. From mountains to marshy flatlands, ancient Iroquoia encompassed a tableau of rugged beauty and rich variety. The crowning assets of this realm were its great forests, consisting primarily of firs and hemlock in the north, and of maple, oak, beech, birch, and elm interspersed with conifers in the south. The forests provided the Iroquoians with an abundance of timber, bark, and woody fibers, which they used to build their homes and canoes and to make sundry household and hunting tools, from wooden bowls and ladles to ropes, bows, and arrow shafts. So critical were the woodlands to Iroquoian life that several species of trees became important religious symbols. The pine, for example, with its evergreen branches, became the symbol of the lasting strength of the Great League.

Lush forest clearings provided the Iroquoians with a variety of edible plants, including skunk cabbage, pokeweed, milkweed, and wild greens. Throughout the summer, women and children gathered wild berries—strawberries, huckleberries, blackberries, and raspberries—spreading them in bark trays to dry under the sun and then storing them away to be baked in breads during the winter. They also harvested various nuts and acorns for food and for oil, along with a native species of hemp, used to fashion lines, nets, and baskets. In the spring, the women collected maple sap, which they boiled into syrup and added as a sweetener to many foods, including the cornmeal that their men carried with them on the warpath and on hunting trips.

The woodlands of Iroquoia also contained plentiful supplies of game animals, from deer and black bears to beavers, rabbits, and muskrats. Hunters tracked bears with specially trained dogs or, in winter, on snowshoes made of wooden strips of white ash, bent and netted with deerhide thongs. The bear hunt involved a long, exhausting, and often dangerous chase, for the idea was to tire the animal before attempting to kill it. The hunters sometimes took bear cubs alive and fattened them in pens for later consumption. Iroquoians put great value on bear meat—which they often served in religious ceremonies—and on bear hides, which they used for blankets. In addition, people covered their bodies with bear grease to provide protection against the cold in the winter and against

Tiny traps made of bark, such as the one below, were used by Iroquoian peoples to snare small birds. Pecking through the hole for kernels of corn left as bait, the bird would catch its neck feathers in a noose made of twined tree fibers, which would tighten as the quarry tried to escape.

In a fanciful European engraving, Canadian Indians fire muskets at beavers near their broken dam. The tidy construction of the dam and the awkward stance of the beavers gnawing on a tree (far right) betray the artist's ignorance of the animal's behavior. But the scene reflects accounts of an early hunting technique in which Indians broke down beaver dams and waited until the animals were swept into the shallows to target them.

insects in the summer. Beavers were another favorite prey of hunters. Men usually pursued these animals in winter when their fur was denser and they could be found at home in their lodges. Brandishing sticks and spears, the hunters sometimes broke through the roofs of the lodges, killing the beavers as they came up for air. Iroquoians made use of almost every part of the animal, from its incisor teeth, which were fashioned into woodworking tools, to its tail, considered a great culinary delicacy.

The chief quarry of Iroquoian hunters, however, was the deer, which served them much as the buffalo served the Plains Indians. Aside from the venison they provided, deer furnished families with hides for clothing, antlers and bones for tools, sinew and gut for bindings, and brains for tanning the hides. Hunters sometimes stalked deer alone in the forest or set traps for them, rigging snares of hemp to bent saplings that snapped up and immobilized the animals. But communal hunts offered the greatest rewards. The Iroquoians often staged elaborate drives in which as many as several hundred people—sometimes including women as well as men—formed a long V-shaped line and marched through the forest, with those at the open ends of the V leading the way. As they advanced, the marchers shook rattles and made other loud noises to drive all the deer within the V toward a river or some other natural obstacle, where hunters waited with bows or spears to dispatch the animals.

Smaller groups of hunters captured a few deer at a time by driving them in a similar manner into triangular wooden enclosures that had been camouflaged in the woods. The French explorer Samuel de Champlain, sojourning among the Huron in 1615, stayed for more than a month with a band of hunters camped near one of these enclosures, where the Indians trapped and killed 120 deer during his stay. Champlain himself joined in the hunt, but he learned the hard way that the tangled forest could be as cruel to strangers as it was generous to the Huron. Losing his way in the woods one day, he had to sleep in the wild for several nights before he spotted smoke from the campfire and found his way back. Thereafter, the chief acting as his host would not let him set foot outside the camp without a Huron companion.

Although deer and other game yielded a host of useful materials, the Huron and several other Iroquoian groups depended for sustenance more on fishing than on hunting. The clear lakes, rivers, and streams of Iroquoia teemed with bass, trout, sturgeon, shad, whitefish, and perch, among other species. In the spring, schools of eel and salmon migrated along the waterways. Throughout the year, groups of men went on fishing expeditions that sometimes lasted a month or more. They used many different techniques, although spearing and netting proved most effective. During the winter, when the lakes froze, the men continued to fish by cutting holes in the ice and dropping nets or hooks on lines into the water. The fish either were eaten fresh or were smoked, dried, and packed in bark containers for later consumption.

The Iroquoians also took fowl in abundance. Although wild turkeys were rare in the northern reaches where the Huron lived, they were plentiful farther south in the homelands of the Five Nations. And huge numbers of migratory game birds, including geese and the now-extinct passenger pigeon, made annual appearances across much of Iroquoia. Men tracked these and other birds to their roosting and nesting areas, where they claimed them with bows and arrows, nets, or snares.

Compared with other Native American peoples, the Iroquoians had few food taboos. About the only animal they universally refused to eat was the snake, which they associated with evil spirits. Otherwise, hunters and foragers were seldom inhibited by legends concerning their potential prey, as was the case in other communities. The turtle, for example, was praised in Iroquoian mythology for offering its back as the foundation on

Worn by a 17th-century Huron chief, this regal out-fit made of sealskin reflects French influences in its tailoring and designs. But Huron embroiderers honored their own tradi-tions by using moose-hair thread and native motifs.

which the earth was constructed. Yet the Huron readily boiled turtles in water or roasted them in hot embers and ate them without compunction.

Nothing the Huron or Iroquois trapped, shot, or netted was as important to their survival as the harvest they claimed from their fields—a legacy of the agricultural revolution that swept across the Northeast beginning about AD 1000. The crops introduced then or soon thereafter—a nutritious triad of corn, beans, and squash that the Iroquois called the Three Sisters—had been domesticated thousands of years earlier in Middle America. From there, the Three Sisters had found their way first to the Southwest, where they nurtured the growth of the Pueblo culture, and later to the Indians settling in large villages along the Mississippi and Ohio rivers. The Iroquoians themselves may then have carried the seeds with them as they migrated to the Northeast and displaced a scattered population of hunter-gatherers.

According to legend, the Three Sisters were a legacy from the Sky Woman, whose fall from heaven led to the formation of the earth and its creatures. After she descended, it was said, she gave birth to a daughter, who in turn gave birth to the Good Twin and then to the Evil Twin—the two brothers responsible for the perpetual struggle between light and darkness. The daughter, who was known to the Iroquois as Our Mother, was said to have died giving birth to the Evil Twin, and from her buried body sprang four plants: tobacco from her head, corn from her heart,

A Seneca woman makes cornmeal by grinding kernels in a hollowed-out tree trunk at New York's Tonawanda Reservation in 1910. Depictions dating back to the 1600s portray Indian women of the region employing similar pestles and mortars.

Working on the porch of their home on New York's Onondaga Reservation, a couple weave cornhusks into bushy strands that later will be coiled into a floor mat. Like other Iroquoians, people of the original Five Nations saw corn as a bequest from patron spirits and made use of every part of the plant—stalks as weapons for boys' war games, cobs as fuel for smoking meat and hides, and silks as hair for cornhusk dolls.

squash from her abdomen, and beans from her fingers. The Good Twin then taught humans how to tend the plants.

The cultivation of corn and other crops defined the Iroquoian way of life. For one thing, it elevated the status of women, who worked the fields and thus became the principal providers within many communities; among some groups, the horticultural work of women contributed up to three-quarters of the food supply. Furthermore, planting furnished tribes with a stable source of food that could be stored through the long winter months, allowing people to live in large villages. Towns of up to 2,000 people eventually became common.

For the most part, the later Iroquoians built their villages not along major waterways, but a mile or two inland, on high ground that afforded protection against enemy attack. They fortified the villages by surrounding them with one or more wooden palisades, composed of timbers lodged securely in the earth and reaching as high as 20 feet into the air. Each palisade had both a front and rear entrance. Scarcely three feet wide, these openings could be easily closed off with logs during an attack. Outside the perimeters of the palisades, the villagers sometimes dug ditches and constructed various earthworks as additional protection. During times of war, they placed enemy scalps on large poles carved to

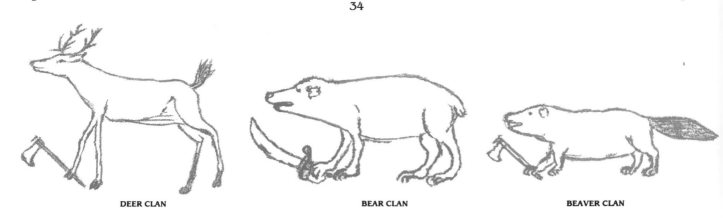

DEER CLAN   BEAR CLAN   BEAVER CLAN

resemble human heads above the front entrance to frighten attackers. European visitors were deeply impressed by these fortress-villages, sometimes referring to them as "castles." Here and there, large villages were surrounded by smaller unfortified hamlets, whose residents might seek refuge within the palisades in times of danger.

Typically, a palisaded village encompassed several acres of land, on which were clustered as many as 60 structures. Most of the buildings were longhouses, the Iroquoians' distinctive form of communal housing. These barnlike dwellings were roughly 18 feet wide and 18 feet tall, and from 40 to 200 feet long. Their windowless walls were framed of saplings set into the ground at about three-foot intervals and then shingled with elm bark fastened together with cordage of woody fibers. Similar materials were used to build the longhouses' vaulted roofs. Screens of bark or hide covered the doorways at each end of the longhouse, and smoke holes that could be closed in bad weather provided ventilation and light at 20-foot intervals along the center of the roof.

Inside the longhouse, underneath each smoke hole, the villagers scooped shallow hearths out of the earthen floor. Each hearth was shared by two "fireside families" of five or six persons who occupied compartments facing each other. Thus, the more fires in a longhouse, the more people the building housed; some contained as many as 12 hearths, or 24 families. Within their compartments, families sat and slept on a low platform that was raised on poles a foot or so off the damp ground and covered with reed or cornhusk mats and blankets of animal pelts. Although bark or hides might be used to screen a family from its neighbors, privacy was minimal. Not surprisingly, some couples preferred to make love in the fields or forests rather than in such close quarters. A Jesuit among the Huron reported that when a village chief was warning his people against sexual relations during a ritual period, he told them "not to go and amuse themselves in the woods."

Iroquoian villages also contained dome-shaped huts for medicinal steam baths and smaller, single-fire houses, occupied by only one or two families—newcomers to the village, perhaps, who could claim no affiliation with the longhouse groups. The families living together within a longhouse were typically members of the same clan who traced their de-

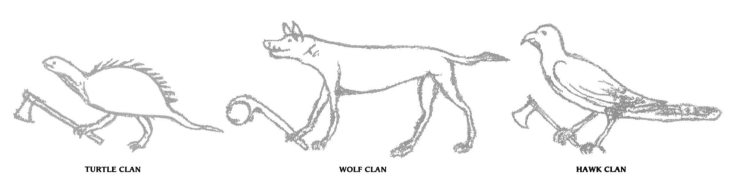

TURTLE CLAN   WOLF CLAN   HAWK CLAN

These emblems, which were copied from tree markings by French travelers during the 1660s, were drawn by the members of an Iroquois war party, who portrayed their various clan symbols clutching weapons, including hatchets, a club, and a sword.

scent through their mothers to a common female ancestor. In practice, this lineage became blurred over the generations, and not all the families in a longhouse were necessarily linked by blood; but they acted as if they were related. Children of either sex inherited the clan affiliation of their mother. Thus a boy belonged to the clan of his mother and lived in the longhouse of his mother's family; but when he grew to manhood and married, his children became members of his wife's clan, not his, and he went to live in the longhouse of his wife's family.

The oldest and most respected woman of a particular family lineage, known as the Clan Mother, presided over the longhouse in which her family lived. Clan membership crossed territorial boundaries. People of the same clan could be found living in many different villages and among several nations. This facilitated travel and communication, for wayfarers were always welcome guests in the longhouses of their clan sisters. Yet because all members of a clan were considered blood relatives, intermarriage among even distant clan members was strictly forbidden.

Each clan claimed a bird or animal as its name and symbol, a carved image of which appeared above the entrance of every longhouse occupied by members of that particular clan. In addition to the carving, the Huron also painted their clan symbols in red on the outer walls of their longhouses. The number of clans represented within a particular nation varied. The Mohawk and the Oneida, for example, had only three clans— Turtle, Wolf, and Bear—while the Huron had those three as well as five others: Beaver, Deer, Hawk, Porcupine, and Snake.

Each clan passed down its own legend of how it came into being. The Snake Clan, for example, told the tale of a young woman who had been secluded in a hut in the woods by her grandmother and instructed to fast so that she would gain special powers from the spirits. After 10 days, a snake appeared to the young woman and spoke to her. "Now you must eat," the snake said, "or I will bring you along with me." Later that night, when her grandmother came to visit, the young woman told of the encounter and asked for food; but her grandmother did not believe her and left her to continue the fast. In time, the snake spirit took hold of the girl and became magically entwined with her. She was lost to her family, but the snake honored her relatives by offering them its shimmering scales as charms and instructing them in dances, songs, and other rituals that brought future members of the clan strength and security.

The women of a clan not only presided over the longhouse and its ceremonies but also claimed ownership of the land, which was normally divided into family plots, part of whose yield was then shared with other members of the clan. When not in their fields, Iroquoian women could be found at the edge of the forest gathering firewood, or in the villages caring for children and making baskets, pots, clothing, and other household objects, including mats, slippers, and dolls woven from cornhusks. Yet according to Mary Jemison, a white woman who was captured as a youngster by the Seneca in the mid-1700s and adopted into the tribe, the work of the women was neither arduous nor interminable. "Our labor was not severe," she insisted after returning to white society. "Notwithstanding the Indian women have all the fuel and bread to procure, and the cooking to perform, their task is probably not harder than that of white women, who have those articles provided for them; and their cares certainly are not half as numerous, nor as great. In the summer season, we planted, tended, and harvested our corn, and generally had all of our children with us; but had no master to oversee or drive us, so that we could work as leisurely as we pleased."

Women performed all the horticultural tasks except one—clearing the fields, which men accomplished by chopping down small trees with stone axes or by girdling large ones; they then burned the fallen branches for firewood, leaving the dead stumps in the ground until they rotted and could be easily removed. Clearing new fields was slow work, and men often began the task several years in advance. A man could clear as much land as he liked for his wife to cultivate, but if one family abandoned a piece of land, another could claim it. In any case, villagers often stored part of the harvest in communal granaries resembling longhouses, and meals were regularly shared. One Dutch visitor to an Iroquois village observed that the chief's longhouse—typically the largest in the village— was the site of frequent meetings and feasts. "In this chief's house, three or four meals were eaten every day," he noted. "Whatever was not cooked there was brought in from other houses in large kettles, because the council came here every day to eat; and whosoever is in the house receives a wooden bowl full of food. If bowls are lacking, then they bring their own bowls and spoons. They then sit down next to one another where the bowls are fetched and brought back full, because an invited guest does not stand up until he has eaten. Sometimes they sing and

Folding and refolding husks, Onondaga craftswoman Molly Velzay perpetuates the venerable art of modeling cornhusk dolls. Recently, graceful creations like the hooded mother and child below have been produced for exhibition and sale, but cornhusk dolls have traditionally served for either the amusement of children or ritual purposes.

sometimes not. Then they thank the host, and each returns home.''

When the soil around a village was exhausted, or when the game and forage were depleted, the villagers moved their entire settlement to a new location. This happened every decade or two. New villages were usually located only a few miles from the old ones so that the men would not have to travel far to clear the fields. An estimated 350 acres of tillable land had to be cleared initially to feed a village of 1,000 people. Men had other neighborhood chores as well. In addition to building the longhouses and palisades—no small tasks—they crafted a variety of useful items, from canoes to animal snares. They also tended to the village's ceremonial tobacco crop, which they grew in small gardens near the longhouses. For much of the year, however, the men were away from the settlements on hunting, trading, or war expeditions. Thus, men mastered the forest, while women dominated the clearings.

The Iroquoians endowed both of those domains with great spiritual power. Whether wild or tame, all things on earth were thought to be possessed of spirits that could either help people or hinder them. The Huron called these supernatural forces *oki,* the most important of which was the one inhabiting the sky and governing the weather, winds, and waves. The sky spirit was invoked by the Huron and other Iroquoians on solemn occasions, such as when concluding a treaty or making a promise. Various groups also held ritual feasts to propitiate the spirits—a curing feast, for example, when a relative had contracted a serious illness, followed by a thanksgiving feast if the person recovered. As a means of keeping in touch with the powers on a daily basis, people made offerings of tobacco and other treasures and observed elaborate rituals and taboos.

Those who neglected such obligations ran the risk of offending the spirits and incurring hunger, sickness, injury, or death. Iroquoian lore is rife with stories of disasters that befell people who slighted the spirits. The Mohawk, for example, attributed the drowning death in 1667 of a Dutch colonist, Arent van Curler, to his refusal to stop at a certain rock on Lake George and offer tobacco to the sky spirit. Deriding his Mohawk companions for what he viewed as a trifling superstition, Curler "turn'd up his back-side toward the rock," as one early English account put it, and instructed his oarsmen to paddle right by the sacred landmark. Minutes later, it was said, a storm swept across the lake, capsizing Curler's canoe and tossing him to his death.

Hunters and fishermen observed special rituals in order to placate their prey. They believed that fish disliked the dead; accordingly, they took pains to store their nets far from the sight of human corpses, and they refrained from fishing too soon after a friend or relative had died. Before casting their nets, Huron men lay on their backs while a shaman addressed the creatures in the lake, reminding them that the Huron respectfully refrained from burning fish bones and asking them to kindly allow themselves to be taken. Before tracking bear or deer, some hunters fasted for a week or more and invoked spiritual aid either by shaking a rattle made from tortoiseshell or by drawing their own blood. Many of the hunters also relied on special charms—perhaps an oddly shaped stone or some object found in the entrails of an animal that had been hunted down. Each of these charms, they believed, hosted a special spirit that would bring them success if they regularly accorded it respect through prayers, songs, or offerings of beads or tobacco.

The spirits of the fields also had to be acknowledged and shown respect. At planting time each spring, as well as at other key moments during the annual growing cycle, villagers gathered to perform special rites designed to please the powers that nurtured their crops. When rain was needed, men might play the rough-and-tumble game of lacrosse. This warlike contest, which evoked the cosmic struggle between good and evil, eventually became part of a formal thunder ceremony among the

THE HEALING POWER OF MEDICINE MASKS

Of all the traditions preserved by the Iroquois Indians, none is more sacred than the healing rituals involving so-called false faces, or medicine masks. So honored are these masks that many Iroquois consider it a sacrilege to photograph them. The use of masks for the curing of ailments has deep roots in the Iroquoian culture: Jesuits entering Huron country in the early 1600s observed many such rituals, including one in which healers wearing wooden masks and disguised as hunchbacks danced around their patients waving sticks. Among the Iroquois, medicine masks have

assumed a spellbinding form, with deep-set eyes and contorted mouths. Many of the masks also display crooked noses to evoke the fabled giant who once challenged the Creator to a test of strength. According to legend, the two sat with their backs to a distant mountain and tried to draw it close by

means of spirit power alone. The giant went first and succeeded in moving the mountain slightly, but the Creator, it is said, summoned it with ease. Turning around to see, the giant smashed his nose against the looming peak. Chastened by defeat, he agreed to protect the Creator's favored children, the Iroquois, from misery and disease if they in turn would promise to honor the giant in their rituals. As illustrated on the following pages, Iroquois mask makers continue to depict the visage of this giant wonder-worker—as well as other healing spirits—for the rites of medicine societies.

Wielding a staff and a rattle and wearing the mask of the legendary giant with his nose askew, a medicine man prepares to drive away sickness in this painting by Iroquois artist Wilfred Chew.

SINGING AWAY SICKNESS

No two medicine masks are alike. Each is shaped by the artist's imagination. Aside from invoking the giant and other healing spirits said to dwell in the forest, Iroquois mask makers sometimes portray supernatural beings that they have encountered in their own dreams or visions.

Their creations figure in a variety of rituals intended not only to prevent disease and heal the sick but also to mark seasonal renewal. Twice each year, in spring and fall, members of Iroquois medicine societies don their masks and run through their villages shaking rattles and brandishing pine boughs as they sweep afflictions from the houses. At the beginning of the midwinter festival, celebrants mask themselves as clowns and beggars and sing and dance, seeking offerings of tobacco and food to honor the protec-

tive spirits. Between ceremonies, society members often perform individual healings, visiting the homes of the afflicted to banish ills.

According to a Seneca legend, the curing power of the false faces was first demonstrated on a dark night long ago, when the Spirit of Sickness slipped through the smoke hole of a longhouse and assailed the inhabitants. The people covered their faces to avoid the deadly gaze of the intruder, but the spirit tried to pull back the covers and peer into their eyes. Just then, the Great False Face—the giant— appeared at the entrance to the longhouse, shaking his rattle and raising a dreadful chant. Terrified, the Spirit of Sickness fled through the smoke hole. Ever since that time, masked medicine men have claimed the power to drive away sickness.

Jake Thomas, a Cayuga carver, begins creating a mask in the traditional manner, roughing out the features before separating the block from the living tree. Before setting to work, carvers burn offerings of tobacco to the spirits and entreat them to grant their masks healing power.

Oneida carver Dick Chrisjohn displays an unfinished mask he has hewn from a section of tree trunk. Once the features are fully sculpted, he will use his tools to open the mouth, rendering the mask sacred.

A finished mask, its metallic eye plates glittering, exudes supernatural strength in this painting by an Iroquois artist. The crooked nose is an indication that the mask invokes the legendary Iroquoian giant and his potent medicine.

Iroquois, performed in late spring or summer to rouse the spirits, who would then release lightning and rain.

One of the oldest and most important of the growth-cycle ceremonies was the Green Corn Ceremony, held in August when the corn was sweet and the first ears would be picked and eaten fresh. Lasting for several days and nights, this festival honored Our Mother and the Good Twin, who had bequeathed corn to the Iroquoians and taught them to cultivate it. The celebration featured special thanksgiving speeches, dances, songs, games, offerings of tobacco, and the naming of babies born since midwinter. A month or two later, the women descended into the fields to harvest the bulk of the corn, a job that included husking the multicolored ears and braiding them into long chains that the women then hung to dry on poles within the longhouses. When the corn and the other crops had

Pictured in 1909, members of a Seneca medicine society gather in their lodge around a doll used during their healing ceremonies. Today, as was the custom in earlier times, the Iroquois have several such societies performing rites that are designed to propitiate the forest creatures and enlist their aid in banishing disease, bringing good fortune, and preventing disasters.

been brought in to sustain the people through the long, cold winter ahead, the villagers held their annual Harvest Festival, several more days of almost nonstop celebrations and feasts.

The most important of the seasonal Iroquoian festivals was one that occurred after the men had returned from their late-autumn hunt. The celebration, which often lasted for more than a week, evidently originated as a response to any prolonged period of sickness or malaise among villagers and later became fixed in midwinter to mark the passage from the old year to the new, or from the season of darkness to the time of light. The specific rites performed during this festival varied from nation to nation. The Seneca sacrificed a small white dog as a symbol of their loyalty to the Good Twin, the bringer of light. Like the Green Corn Festival, the midwinter rite also served as a time for naming children born in the past half-year. Babies received their names from a pool of titles reserved for a particular clan and not currently in use; when the youngster reached adulthood, that name was often exchanged for another that evoked a spirit or quality the individual was expected to live up to.

Among the Huron, the midwinter rite took on a frenzied tone. Known as Ononharoia, or the "Upsetting of the Brain," the ceremonies began at night when groups of villagers disturbed by anxious thoughts or dreams of longing ran from longhouse to longhouse, making noise and overturning the furnishings. During the commotion, houses sometimes caught fire. The following day, the people who had feigned madness returned to the longhouses to ask the residents at each hearth to guess the nature of dreams they had experienced the night before and to give them the object that their dreams indicated they desired—a pipe, perhaps, or a kettle or an animal pelt. To help the guessers, the dreamers gave hints in the form of riddles. Someone who wanted to elicit a gift of a glass bead, for example, might say, "What I see in my eyes, it will be marked with various colors." In the Huron language, a single word meant both "eye" and "glass bead." After listening to the riddles, the guesser placed an object in front of the dreamer. If the guess was incorrect, the dreamer moved to another hearth, taking along the already-guessed items to make it easier for the next family to narrow down the possibilities.

When someone finally presented the dreamer with the desired object, the dreamer gave a cry of joy and gratitude and rushed out of the house, his or her mind and body now free of the burden. Outside, people congratulated the dreamer by striking their hands on the ground and shouting, "He, e, e, e, e!" Near the conclusion of the ceremony, groups of

dreamers went into the forest to exorcise any lingering disturbance. When they reemerged from the woods, they returned all the items they had received from the villagers during the dream guessing, except the objects they had specifically desired.

Underlying this guessing game was a conviction that thwarted wishes were the cause of serious and sometimes fatal maladies. When members of the community fell ill, their neighbors and kin did all they could to fulfill the individuals' desires as revealed in their dreams. A sick man who dreamed of a certain young woman, for example, might be permitted to consort with her if she was free. In one instance, a sick woman dreamed that she would be healed if she received the pet cat given to the chief of her village by a French priest. The chief fulfilled her wish, in spite of the fact that his own daughter had grown attached to the animal. Subsequently, the girl grew despondent and died.

Curing was difficult if patients were unaware of their thwarted desires or unable to express them. In such cases, a medicine man would be called in to divine the wish. If he sensed that the patient was beyond help, he diagnosed a secret longing that could not possibly be fulfilled. But usually the medicine man peered into the patient's soul and discerned a wish that could be satisfied at least in part. Extravagant desires were sometimes allayed with substitutes. One patient who dreamed of four beavers, for example, had to be content with four large fish. In addition to these

In a photograph taken about 1900, a man watches two women on the Onondaga Reservation play an age-old Iroquois game of chance using a bowl and six dicelike peach pits, colored black on one side and white on the other (opposite). The contest, which involves striking the bowl on the ground in the hope of getting at least five pits to come up black or white, once matched village against village; each side chose a player, who relied on a special ritual or charm for success, and wagered on the outcome.

wish-fulfillment cures, various remedies were administered by members of medicine societies, who sometimes drew their own blood or danced with hot stones or live embers in their hands to cast out afflictions.

When treatment failed and a person died, Iroquoian communities signaled their solidarity by relieving the bereaved clan of the burden of conducting the funeral. Clans were part of larger social entities, which the Iroquoians referred to as "groups of sisters and brothers." Typically, there were two such groups, called moieties, or halves. The Seneca, for example, had one moiety that was composed of the clans named for four-footed animals, with the exception of the Deer Clan; the other included the Deer Clan and all clans named for birds. Just as people could not intermarry within their clan, they also could not intermarry within this larger group. Although the moieties sometimes competed in festivals, they cooperated in times of mourning. People of one group prepared the deceased of another for burial and offered condolences, enabling the bereaved relatives to focus on their grief.

Iroquoians buried their dead either in the ground, with stakes or an earthen mound to mark the spot, or in a bark coffin set on a raised platform some eight to 10 feet off the ground. Everyone in the village prepared food for the friends and relatives of the deceased and ate it during a wakelike ceremony that the Huron called the Feast of Souls. People also brought presents of clothing, tools, and other items. Mourners placed some of these gifts—perhaps a few beads, a comb, or a gourd of oil— inside the grave with the deceased to help the soul make a successful journey to the land of the dead. Iroquoians believed, however, that a second spirit—the ghost of the deceased—remained near the village, wandering through the longhouses at night and eating what remained of the evening meal. For this reason, many Iroquoian speakers would not eat food that had been left standing overnight, which they considered the food of the dead and thus poisonous if consumed by the living.

Among the Huron, every time a large village moved to a new location—and after 12 years or so if the community remained in place that long—the people in the vicinity held a unique commemorative rite called the Feast of the Dead. At that time, the bones of all who had died during the period—except those who

Tending to an ailing neighbor, three men in medicine masks perform a curing ceremony in a painting by Iroquois artist Rick Hill. The healer at right rubs hot ashes on the patient's arm, while the medicine man at left frightens away the evil spirits that cause illness by shaking a turtle-shell rattle.

had suffered a violent death and were considered dangerous—were uncovered and reburied in a common pit, or ossuary. The women prepared the bodies for the 10-day ceremony, stripping any remaining flesh from the bones of all but the most recently buried bodies and wrapping them in beaver skins. Witnesses to this procedure reported that the women worked solemnly and without any sign of disgust, no matter how putrid the remains. The men then placed the wrapped bones on litters and carried them to the main village hosting the feast.

At the ossuary, the skeleton bundles were first draped over poles; the bones were then mingled in the pit to unite the souls for their journey to the next world, where they would reside together. Once the remains had been covered over, a lavish exchange of presents took place to honor the dead. Jesuits who witnessed the Feast of the Dead in 1636 reported that more than 1,200 presents, most of them beaver robes, were exchanged by the participants. Afterward, the relatives of the deceased, satisfied that their loved ones had received an honorable farewell, held a joyous feast.

Such ceremonies reflected a powerful sense of community. Iroquoians of various nations cultivated this spirit of solidarity through political customs that bridged the gaps between clans and between the sexes. Each clan segment within a village appointed its own chiefs who spoke for the clan at village councils. The chiefs were men, but they were chosen and advised by the prominent women of their lineage, led by the Clan Mother. One French missionary observed that the women "were always the first to deliberate on private and community matters. They hold their councils apart and, as a result of their decisions, advise the chiefs." In consultation with the women, the chiefs would approve the headman, or leader of the village. Sometimes a headman who died would be succeeded by a relative—usually, a sister's son. But no village leader held a birthright to his position. If he failed to live up to the community's expectations, he could be replaced at the prompting of the council chiefs and the women advising them.

Like many other Native American cultures, the Iroquoians had separate civil chiefs and war chiefs. The civil council always met in the longhouse of the headman, but the war council sometimes gathered in a secluded spot in the forest to maintain secrecy. In both cases, chiefs initiated the discussions, but others could and did attend, and everyone present was given an opportunity to speak. War councils were called to initiate raids or defend against enemy predations. Civil councils addressed such issues as whether to build a new longhouse, or how to settle disputes between families of different clans; special weight was given to the opinions of a group of wise elders known as the Old Men. Once the councilmembers arrived at a consensus, the headman announced their decision to the village. Leaders had no power to demand compliance; they could only persuade and cajole. Indeed, a headman who tried to impose his will on his followers ran the risk of losing their respect—and his job. Yet those renowned for their eloquence and good judgment commanded fierce support from their followers. In one case, Jesuits had to intervene to protect a young Huron who impulsively struck a revered leader and was pounced on by his fellow villagers.

From time to time, councils were called upon to mete out punishment

ANCIENT WAYS OF MAKING MUSIC

In their festivities, the Iroquois have long relied on an ingenious array of instruments to "prop up the songs." Most are rhythm instruments, including water drums, whose tone depends on the level of liquid inside, and various rattles, made of gourd, bark, horns, or deer dewclaws—the vestigial hoofs at the back of the animals' legs. For melody, Iroquois musicians use wooden flutes, which are traditionally played more for diversion than for ceremonial purposes.

FOLDED HICKORY-BARK RATTLE

GOURD RATTLE WITH WOODEN HANDLE

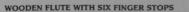
WOODEN FLUTE WITH SIX FINGER STOPS

DEER-DEWCLAW RATTLES FOR TYING AROUND LEGS

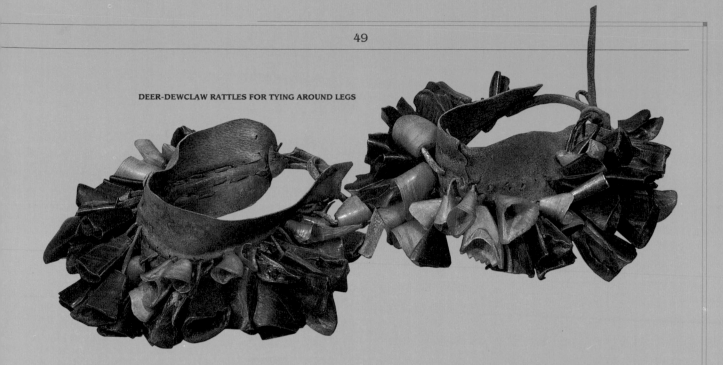

WATER DRUM OF WOOD AND LEATHER

COW-HORN RATTLE WITH WOODEN HANDLE

to wrongdoers. Those guilty of theft or causing injury typically had to compensate the victim with animal furs or other valued property. If the injured person held a position of prestige in a nearby village, a feast might be given in his or her honor by the village of the assailant. The members of the community would then keep a close eye on the offender to ensure that the crime was not repeated, bringing with it the expense of another feast. More serious offenses, in particular witchcraft and treason, customarily drew a sentence of death, which the council enacted by announcing that the accused now stood outside the law and that anyone could kill him or her without fear of reprisal. In theory, the mere accusation that a person had used evil charms to bring harm to another was enough to support a charge of witchcraft. A sick man might dream that one of his neighbors had bewitched him, for example, and if the victim was taken at his word, his alleged tormentor would be subject to the death penalty. In practice, however, council chiefs considered the character of the accused before passing sentence. Those condemned to die as witches usually had a record of selfish or disruptive behavior that had alienated them from their fellow villagers.

Although murder was considered a heinous crime, it was not punished with death. Instead, council chiefs required the murderer—and often his neighbors and kin—to offer extravagant presents to the family of the deceased. Among the Huron, the village of the murderer might be ordered to offer the village of the victim up to 60 presents, each of them equal to or greater than a beaver robe in value. The typical assessment, however, was 30 such presents for the murder of a man and 40 presents for the murder of a woman—an amount that reflected the high value placed on women as nurturers and providers. Such fines were imposed to avert the prolonged blood feuds that resulted when a family, clan, or village took upon itself the responsibility of avenging the death of one of its own by attacking the murderer or his kin.

Although the Huron and the Iroquois managed to suppress such feuds internally, vengeance remained a prime motive for strife between those two groups and between other rivals in the region. Only as European influence increased and fur trading became more important for the Iroquoians did economic competition contribute significantly to their conflicts. Traditionally, war served them not as a means of gaining territory or controlling trade routes, but as a way of acquiring prestige and achieving retribution—an end that was best accomplished by taking prisoners to compensate for earlier losses to the enemy. Some of the prison-

Hurons celebrate their solemn Feast of the Dead, performed periodically by communities to gather the remains of the deceased in a common grave so that their souls could travel together to the next world. Although this 18th-century French engraving captures the communal spirit of the rite, it errs in portraying whole corpses being lugged to the site and skeletons dangling from the scaffold. In fact, the bones of the deceased were wrapped in beaver hide until the time came to mingle them in the pit.

ers were adopted, but others were sacrificed in agonizing rites that saw villagers abandon their customary restraint and vent the rage that their communal codes otherwise kept in check.

Typically, a raid of retribution was instigated by the relatives of a person slain by the enemy. Those mourners called for vengeance by presenting gifts to their village war chiefs. If the chiefs agreed that an attack on the enemy was justified, they made a declaration at the victim's funeral that the murder must not go unanswered. The war chiefs then sought volunteers for the war party from within the village as well as from neighboring settlements, often traveling from place to place dispensing gifts of their own. Support came most readily from the younger men, who welcomed war as an opportunity to exhibit their bravery and thereby increase their standing within the tribe.

When enough recruits had been gathered, the war chiefs called a council at which the decision was confirmed. A war feast followed that evening. The women served the warriors platters of dog meat and the broth in which it was cooked, symbolizing the flesh and blood of enemy prisoners who would be taken. The leading warriors received the heads of the dogs. Then the dancing and singing began to the accompaniment of drums and rattles, the warriors twisting and bending their bodies in motions that imitated the actions of battle. Before a battle, warriors also made offerings of tobacco to the war spirit, praying for a successful raid, the capture of many prisoners, and a safe return. Among the Huron, the war spirit sometimes appeared to the warrior as a dwarf in a dream. If the dwarf caressed the warrior, it foretold victory, but if the spirit struck the man on the forehead, he knew to prepare for death. Iroquoian warriors also consulted shamans before setting out on a raid, asking them to peer into the future and predict the outcome of the impending fight.

When several villages and hamlets combined to form a war party, they could easily muster several hundred men or more. The warriors of-

A finely modeled head, complete with a metal earring and a tattoo on its cheek, forms the bowl of a soapstone pipe carved by an Indian artisan in or around Iroquois country after trade with Europeans began. Iroquoians had smoked tobacco ceremonially in pipes such as these since ancient times.

ten started out together but usually divided into furtive groups of five or six once they entered enemy territory. For the most part, Iroquoian fighting men preferred covert raids to open battles, and although they often fought bravely when challenged, they considered it foolish to struggle to the last man without hope of prevailing.

When war parties did clash, they traded shots with bows and arrows from a distance, then moved in for close combat wielding ball-headed war clubs. More often, raiders sneaked up on isolated groups of people working in the fields or foraging and either killed and scalped them on the spot or took them prisoner. Knowing the treatment that awaited them, some who were attacked chose to fight to the death. Others threw off their wampum necklaces and ran, hoping that their pursuers would stop to pick up the prized ornaments, giving them time to escape.

When a returning war party neared one of its villages, the warriors sounded special whoops and cries from the forest to announce their successes or losses. Prisoners were handed over to the war chiefs, who met in council to determine which clan segment they should be given to. Captive women and children were often adopted by families to replace lost relatives. But male prisoners had to endure a period of agonizing uncertainty as their captors decided how to dispose of them. The decision was purely subjective; if a prisoner's demeanor or abilities pleased his guardians, they might choose to let him live and become part of their family. A prisoner condemned to die, however, was also formally adopted by his captors, who addressed him as "brother" or "nephew" and spoke words of affection to him even as they prepared him for his terrible fate. The women wept when they fed him, and the men shared their tobacco pipe with him and wiped the sweat from his face.

The torture ceremony, which could last several days, began with a farewell feast, during which the prisoner sang songs and showed his courage by walking up and down the longhouse, inviting his captors to kill him. Prisoners always looked for opportunities to flee—some were forced to walk on live coals as part of their ordeal and took the occasion to kick the embers aside, starting fires or raising smoke that gave them a slim chance to escape. Barring that, they behaved as bravely as possible throughout the gruesome event, knowing it reflected well on their people and frustrated their tormentors; the Iroquois considered it an evil omen if their victims failed to weep and beg for mercy. Such stoicism must have been extremely difficult to sustain, however, for the torture was both grisly and unrelenting. Prisoners had their fingernails torn out, their bones broken, and their ears pierced with burning sticks. They received scalding burns and deep cuts on all parts of their bodies. Their tormentors, who included both men and women, mocked them continuously throughout the ceremony, trying to get them to break down.

The execution of prisoners always came after dawn, for the Iroquoians thought it important that the sun, identified with the Good Twin, be on hand to witness the destruction of evil ones. The captors led their victim to a scaffold erected outside the village's palisade. There, the prisoner suffered his final agonies. His captors blinded his eyes with a burning stick, scalped him, and forced him to eat pieces of his own flesh. When the victim was near death, his captors either cut off his head or broke it open with a club. They then cut

An Iroquois war captive is tortured with fire in this stylized drawing by a 17th-century Dutch voyager to New Netherland, near Mohawk country. Iroquoians sometimes ended such rites by consuming part of the victim's flesh, leading Algonquian-speaking Indians of New England to dub the Iroquois nearest to them Mohowawog, or "Man-eaters"—a term the English abridged to Mohawk.

open his body and distributed his entrails to children, who hung them on the ends of sticks and marched triumphantly through the village. If the prisoner had shown exceptional bravery, the young men would roast and eat his heart in the hope of acquiring some of his courage.

Such frightful ordeals inevitably provoked calls for retaliation from the victim's friends and kin, who found it difficult to put aside their grief until a similar punishment had been inflicted on one of the enemy. Before the formation of the Iroquois and Huron alliances, blood feuds marked by acts of cannibalism and visceral brutality must have frequently set clan against clan, tribe against tribe. Archaeological findings suggest that such carnage escalated as the Iroquoians became more reliant on horticulture and congregated in larger settlements, with the violence reaching a peak about 1500. Evidently, men whose hunting activities were no longer of great importance to the welfare of the community turned increasingly to fighting and feuding as ways of acquiring prestige.

Fortunately, the Iroquoians also possessed a strong tradition of alliance building that helped leaders control the violent impulses within tribes and confederacies, if not between them. Aside from the clan ties that transcended local boundaries, trade was a time-honored instrument of conciliation. The Iroquoians regarded trade as a test of friendship in which each side honored the other with gifts. Such amicable exchanges often helped potential rivals overcome formidable barriers of language and custom; the Huron, for example, maintained peaceful relations with their Algonquian trading partners even as they feuded with the Iroquois. In the founding legend of the Iroquois League, when Deganawida consoled Hiawatha with the gift of wampum, he was teaching embattled peoples to trade courtesies instead of blows. This ritual of peacemaking was not confined to members of the league. On one occasion, after some Huron villagers murdered a French priest, the village chiefs compensated his fellow missionaries by offering them wampum and other prizes. At the exchange, the Huron used words that echoed the speech of Deganawida to the grieving Hiawatha: "We wipe away your tears by this gift."

Just when this peacemaking process among the Iroquoians led to intertribal alliances remains uncertain. The peoples known collectively as the Huron evidently came to an understanding sometime in the 16th century, and the Five Nations of the Iroquois probably concluded their great peace about the same time. A Seneca legend may offer a clue as to the date of the accord. The tale says that the Seneca were about to be attacked by the neighboring Mohawk in retaliation for an earlier raid when "the sun went out, and for a little while it was complete darkness." The Seneca took this as a message from the spirits that their blood feud with the Mohawk should end and so conciliated that tribe and joined in the great peace. The darkness referred to may simply be symbolic of the evil afflicting people in those times, but the legend says it descended during the last tilling of the corn crop—circumstances consistent with eclipses of the sun that took place on June 28, 1451, and again on June 18, 1536.

The laws of the great peace that were attributed to Deganawida and Hiawatha did more than simply proclaim harmony among the Five Nations—they established ceremonies and conventions that preserved the peace. Every year representatives of the Five Nations came together in the Grand Council to reaffirm their accord and allay any ill feelings between the members. "There all the deputies from the different nations are present," a French missionary wrote of this council in 1668, "to make their complaints and receive the necessary satisfaction in mutual gifts, by means of which they maintain a good understanding with one another."

The Grand Council was not set up to declare war or approve treaties. Those matters remained the prerogatives of the separate nations and their village chiefs. To be sure, chiefs from two or more of the Five Nations often met separately to reach accords on matters of war, trade, or diplomacy, and in that sense, the Iroquois formed a loose confederacy, whose concerns later came to dominate meetings of the council. But the original mission of the Iroquois League and its Grand Council was to maintain a spirit of peace and goodwill among the Five Nations.

The Grand Council persisted as an institution into the 20th century, and its procedures were thus well documented. In all, there were 50 positions, or titles, on the council, each of which bore the name of one of the league's original chiefs—including the legendary Hiawatha and Atotarho, although the council always left the position of Hiawatha unfilled. The other titles were assigned to the various clans within each of the Five Nations, with some clans receiving more than one title. The Onondaga, who had eight clans, warranted 14 titles, while the other nations, with fewer clans, claimed fewer titles.

That one nation had more positions on the council than another was of little consequence, because the members did not vote—they deliberated and sought a consensus. The meetings were always held in the land of the Onondaga, the Keepers of the Central Fire, and were presided over by an Onondaga worthy who went by the dreaded name of Atotarho but exerted no special power over the group. Participants sat in the council house around a large fire, ar-

A maple-wood cane, used during the condolence rites of the Great League of Peace to call the roll of the chiefs, is inscribed with symbols of the league's 50 ancestral titles. Pegs at the edge of the cane designate nine titles for the Mohawk (far left)—three for each of the nation's three clans—nine positions for the Oneida, 14 for the Onondaga, 10 for the Cayuga, and eight for the Seneca.

ranged by nation and divided into two moieties. One moiety, called the Elder Brothers, consisted of the Onondaga, Mohawk, and Seneca. The Oneida and Cayuga formed the other moiety, known as the Younger Brothers. After offering prayers and songs to commemorate the founding of the league, councilmembers rose to speak. Often, the debate concerned an internal dispute, such as restitution for a crime committed by the member of one nation against the member of another. As each councilmember spoke, he held in his hands a belt of wampum, which he hung on a pole for everyone to see when he was finished. The wampum belt signified that what he said was true. It also served to refresh the memories of later speakers, who could review point by point—or wampum by wampum—the arguments made by their predecessors.

Because council decisions had to be unanimous, the debates often continued for days, requiring considerable patience and diplomacy of the participants. The council suspended its meetings each evening, believing it unwise to discuss important matters at night when the Evil Twin, the force of darkness, came out to reign. If the chiefs failed to reach a consensus on an issue, they doused the council fire with ashes, a symbolic act signifying their inability to "roll their words into one bundle." The chiefs then returned to their own villages without taking any action.

Aside from this annual gathering, the Grand Council convened on special occasions as well—most notably the death of a councilmember, at which time his clan appointed a new titleholder to be "raised up" in his place. The burial of the old chief and the raising up of the new was marked by a solemn ritual known as the Condolence Ceremony. As in the village when someone died, the moiety unrelated to the deceased arranged the details for the burial and ceremony. Thus, if the deceased had belonged to the Elder Brothers, the duty of hosting the ceremony fell to the Younger Brothers, whose condolences echoed those of Deganawida when he soothed Hiawatha and lifted away his grief. "The speaker addresses the mourners as his children," one witness to the Condolence Ceremony observed. "He wipes away their tears that they may see clearly; he opens their ears that they may hear readily. He removes from their throats the obstruction with which their grief is choking them, so that they may ease their burdened minds by speaking freely to their friends."

In the early days of the league, this compelling ritual, and similar observances among the Huron, helped preserve harmony within those alliances at times of bereavement, when grief and rage might otherwise have sundered their bonds. But no peacemaker emerged to reconcile the Iroquois to the Huron, or to others they perceived as their mortal enemies. Instead, the provocative presence of Europeans and their wares intensified ancestral rivalries and ushered the Iroquois into a stormy new season of peril and mourning. ◆

THE COMMUNAL SHELTER

In the world of the Iroquois, nothing expressed the idea of community more than the longhouse. Just as the nations of the Iroquois League lived geographically linked in union, so did Iroquois families dwell side by side in longhouses. A traveler crossing ancient Iroquoia passed along the Iroquois Trail through a symbolic longhouse that stretched from the Hudson River valley to Lake Erie. The families of an

The village of Garoga—the Mohawk name for a nearby creek—was built on a steep-sided, 2½-acre bluff 150 feet high. Protected on three sides by ravines and on the west by a stout palisade, the longhouses were sited to fit the topography. Later, after the Europeans came, villages were often arranged geometrically, the houses aligned in rows and surrounded by a rectangular palisade.

actual longhouse lived in compartments accessible by a central corridor that evoked the overland passage.

Typical of these dwellings were the structures at Garoga, a community of some 800 Mohawks containing nine longhouses, each home to 16 to 20 related families. Like most Iroquois villages, Garoga was probably occupied for less than two decades. When the land surrounding it was exhausted by cultivation, perhaps between 1525 and 1550, the villagers took up their belongings and moved on to another site. The ridge on which the village stood was soon reclaimed by the for-

est. What had been Garoga was concealed from human view until the late 19th century, when amateur collectors searching New York's countryside for Indian relics discovered the potsherds, beads, animal bones, tools, and weapons that had been discarded.

Decades later, archaeologists found more evidence of village life there: impressions of hundreds of storage pits and post molds in the loamy soil, defining the contours and dimensions of this Iroquois community. The artist's renderings of Garoga on these pages are based on that evocative earthen blueprint of the town.

BUILDING A LONGHOUSE

Garoga was probably built over the span of a year or two, as villagers left their former homes in groups and moved into the new settlement. Each year, as the sap rose at winter's end, builders peeled thick sheaths of bark from elm trees, flattened the bark into sheets, and dried them in stacks weighted with stones to prevent warping. The flattened sheets were then used as siding and roof shingles.

Iroquois builders usually framed the houses in April and May. They sank peeled elm poles as thick as a man's calf deep into the ground in parallel rows, about 18 feet apart, that extended the projected length of the building—from 40 to 200 feet or more, depending on the number of families that would live there. About 10 feet above the ground, they lashed on stabilizing cross poles and green saplings, bent into rafters that arched across the width of the structure. They then laid on the bark shingles, securing them to the frame with lightweight poles tied horizontally at intervals along the roof.

Often, they added a vestibule for storage at the end of the longhouse, with a small porch to shelter the door. They built this annex less sturdily than the main structure so they could readily pull it down and extend the longhouse to accommodate additional families. Similarly, when the Iroquois brought new peoples into their league, it was said, "the rafters are extended."

CLAY COOKING POT

A SHARED INTERIOR

Elm-bark boards, like those used to sheathe the longhouse exterior, divided the interior into the two-family compartments in which the residents lived. Builders placed these interior walls about 18 to 20 feet apart, framing generous doors six to eight feet wide in each partition to leave a broad, open center aisle running the length of the structure. Additional interior framework supported bark-covered sleeping and sitting platforms a couple of feet off the ground and storage areas built at a height of about seven feet.

Other than the minimal ventilation offered by the doors at each end, the only light and air to enter a longhouse came through the smoke holes centered above the shared hearth in each compartment. The atmosphere beneath those sooty apertures was close to suffocating—a dark miasma of pungent odors and smoky air so particle laden that many Iroquois suffered from serious respiratory and eye ailments. In 1616 French explorer Samuel de Champlain reported that numerous elderly longhouse residents had lost their sight as a consequence of the unwholesome air of their dwellings.

WOVEN SALT CONTAINER

THE DOMESTIC SPACE

The Iroquois nuclear family generally consisted of a mother and father and two to four children. Occupying one-half of a typical longhouse compartment, they shared a domestic space consisting of a series of open-sided cubicles. The largest of these was the elevated sleeping platform, approximately six to eight feet long. Covered with animal skins and cornhusk mats, this broad bench functioned as a bed for the entire family at night and as a seating area during the day.

Storage sections abutted the sleeping cubicle. Families kept caches of treasured personal items, such as smoking pipes and wampum beads, in pits dug beneath the platform. The large ground-level sections on either side held necessities of daily life—firewood, corn, beans, squash, and other foodstuffs in bark barrels—as well as ongoing projects, such as unworked hides or half-finished beadwork. The upper platform served as the family attic, the repository of tools, weapons, and stocks of trade goods such as animal pelts. High above, tied to rafters and crossbeams, hung braided bunches of corn and strips of dried fish.

CORN-WASHING BASKET

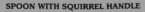
SPOON WITH SQUIRREL HANDLE

To create a wampum string (above, center), an artisan hammered off portions of a seashell (top left). He then clamped each fragment into a wooden vise (left) and shaped it on a grindstone. The cylindrical shell beads were then pierced with a bow-powered drill (right).

The Hiawatha wampum belt (above) commemorates the founding of the confederacy and serves as its constitution. At its center, the Onondaga Nation, capital of the league, appears as the Great Tree of Peace. The squares represent the other league members.

THE IMPORTANCE OF WAMPUM

Wampum, tiny beads fashioned from seashells, played a major role in Iroquois life. Woven into belts and other articles, wampum served as a currency during the heyday of the fur trade, but its value to the Iroquois and neighboring tribes was more spiritual than monetary. Wampum, in reality, evoked the very founding of the Iroquois confederacy. According to legend, the Onondaga chief Hiawatha, mourning the deaths of his wife and daughters, met the prophet Deganawida, who consoled the grieving

man with strings of white shells. (The word *wampum* is derived from an Algonquian phrase meaning "strings of white.") The two men, bonded in friendship, worked together to forge the league of tribes.

Possessing a rich oral tradition but no written alphabet, the Iroquois used the beads as memory aids to record tribal history and sacred pacts. They first traded for wampum with coastal tribes, who used conch and quahog shells to craft the white beads, signifying purity, and the purple ones, which stood for grief. White beads reddened with ocher symbolized war. The belt's design also held a message: A row of diamonds, for example, might mean friendship, while squares might

signify council fires. The information conveyed by the colors and designs of wampum documents was memorized by tribal wampum keepers, or historians.

Wampum was also essential to diplomacy between the Iroquois and the Europeans. Before treaty talks, the Iroquois exchanged wampum as a sign of sincerity. When a pact was made, its terms were woven into a belt, and the agreement was sealed by a gift of wampum. Although many wampum objects are now possessed by non-Indian collectors and museums, the Iroquois have begun to reclaim this vital part of their heritage by successfully negotiating the return of a host of items, including more than two dozen belts.

SYMBOLS
OF DIPLOMACY

The Wing belt (right), named for its design, is displayed whenever the Iroquois constitution is read; the purple chevrons were not meant to depict wings but rather a pine tree growing without limit, a metaphor signifying that peace will endure as long as the confederacy exists.

The wampum string above was used to invite the chiefs of one village to a meeting in another. The attached stick was notched to show the days remaining before the meeting.

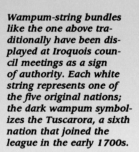

Wampum-string bundles like the one above traditionally have been displayed at Iroquois council meetings as a sign of authority. Each white string represents one of the five original nations; the dark wampum symbolizes the Tuscarora, a sixth nation that joined the league in the early 1700s.

Amid statesmen from the other Iroquois nations, Onondaga chief David John, Sr. (center), holds the tribal string bundle at a council meeting in about 1910 in the Six Nations Council House in Ontario, Canada.

PRIZED OFFERINGS

Wampum was so highly prized by the Iroquois that personal ornaments such as the armlet shown here were as treasured as items created for political and religious reasons.

In 1678 Christianized Hurons made the belt below as a gift for Chartres Cathedral, where it now hangs. Its Latin words mean "Offering of the Huron to the Virgin with Child."

The prized wampum
medallion at right
was given to signify
open and honest
diplomatic relations.
The white circle
stands for the sun.

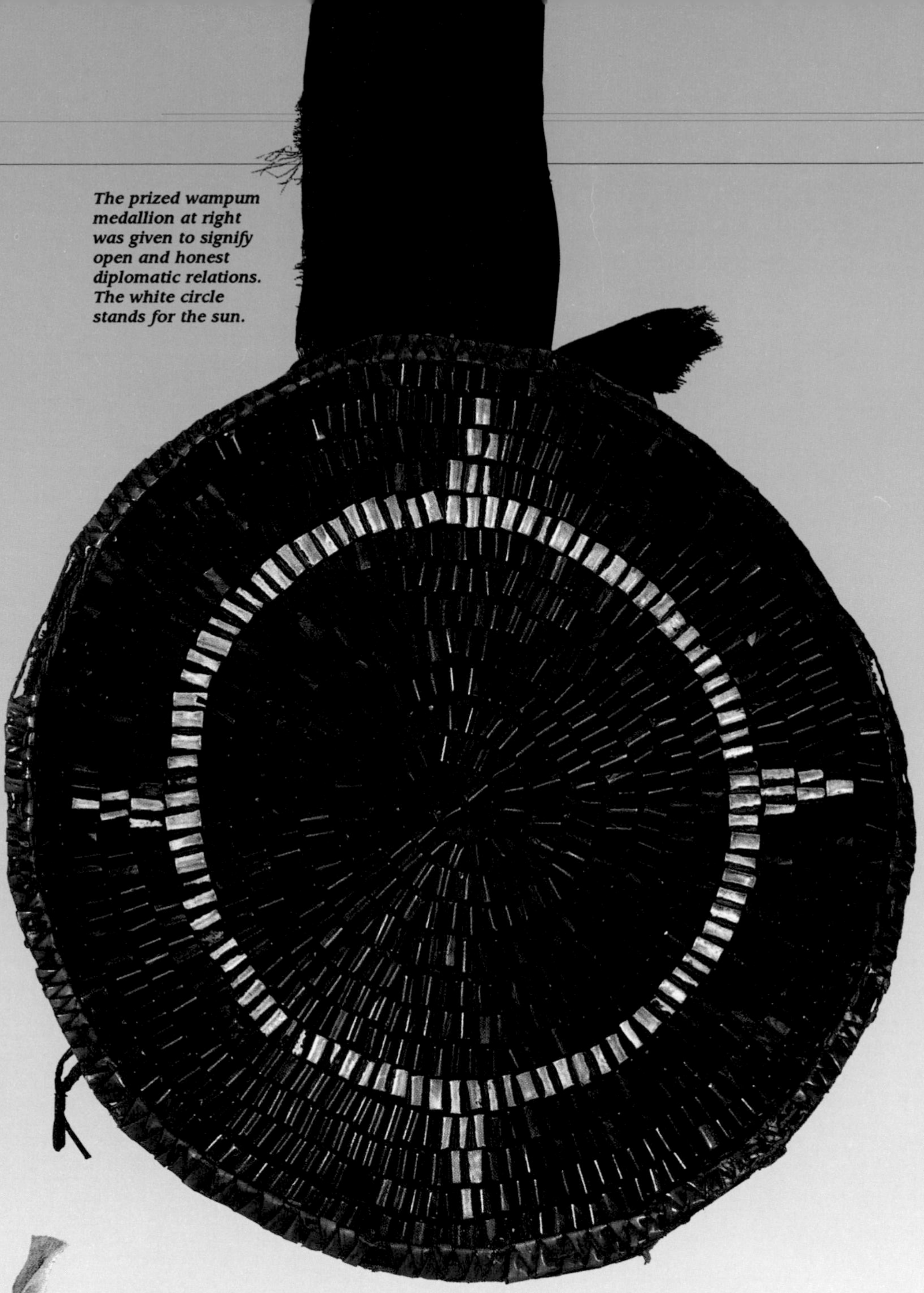

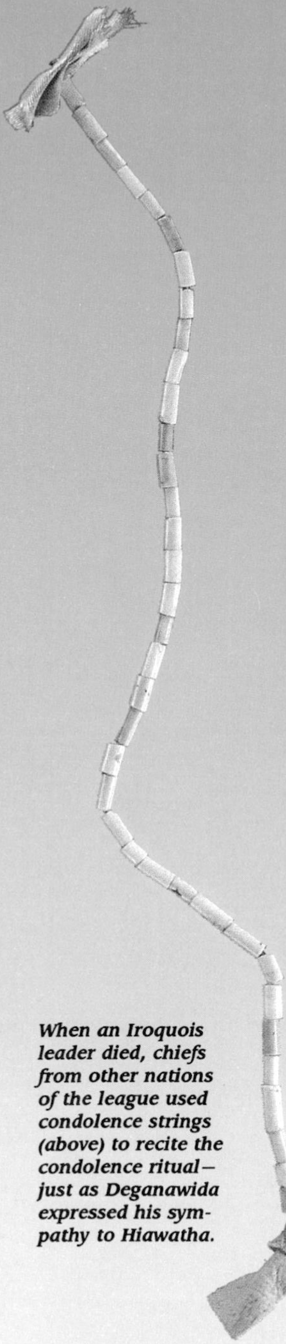

When an Iroquois
leader died, chiefs
from other nations
of the league used
condolence strings
(above) to recite the
condolence ritual—
just as Deganawida
expressed his sym-
pathy to Hiawatha.

BEADED COVENANTS

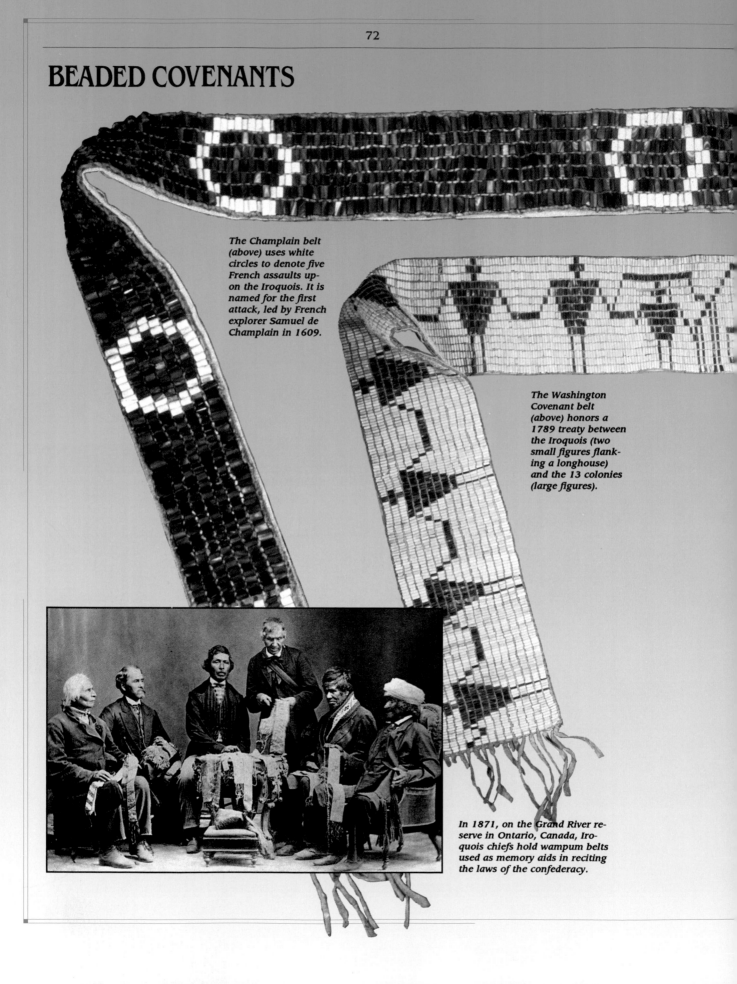

The Champlain belt (above) uses white circles to denote five French assaults upon the Iroquois. It is named for the first attack, led by French explorer Samuel de Champlain in 1609.

The Washington Covenant belt (above) honors a 1789 treaty between the Iroquois (two small figures flanking a longhouse) and the 13 colonies (large figures).

In 1871, on the Grand River reserve in Ontario, Canada, Iroquois chiefs hold wampum belts used as memory aids in reciting the laws of the confederacy.

In 1611 the Huron requested an alliance with France by presenting what is now called the Four Nations belt (right) to Champlain. It depicts shield-bearing Huron warriors.

THE RETURN
OF THE BELTS

The Atotarho belt (below), named for the legendary Onondaga chief, was returned to the Iroquois Indians by the New York State Museum in 1988. At council meetings, the belt confirmed the traditional role of the Onondaga as keepers of the council fire.

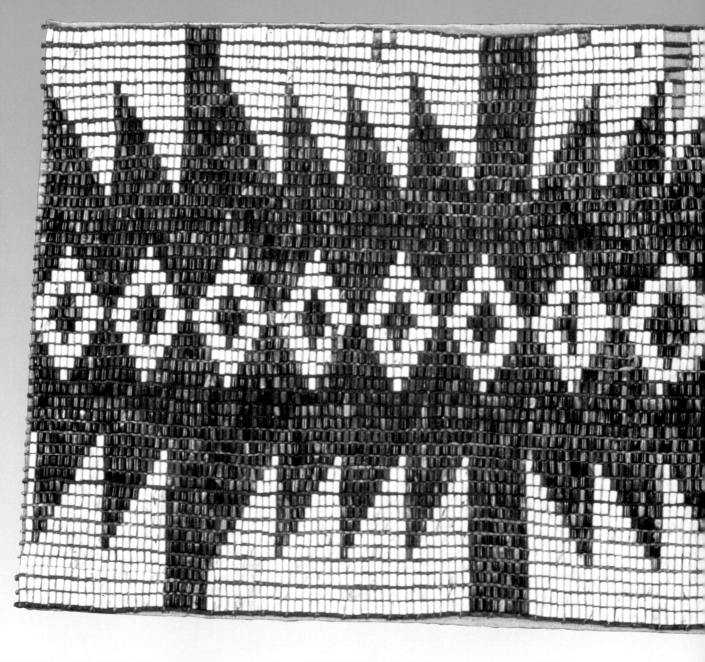

At a 1988 ceremony at the Grand River reserve, Roland Force of the Museum of the
American Indian and Cayuga chief Jake
Thomas examine several belts returned to
the Iroquois by the museum. The French
Peace belt, honoring an Iroquois accord
with French settlers, is second from right.

In a detail from the French
Peace belt (above), the verti-
cal line represents the way
of peace, while the solid dia-
mond is one of several that
stand for French settlements.
Elsewhere on the belt are
open diamonds signifying the
nations of the league.

2

THE EUROPEAN INTRUSION

In an 18th-century engraving by a French artist, a stylized Iroquois warrior displays a collection of Iroquois accouterments, including a war club, bead strings, and unseasonal snowshoes. The figure's cruel expression epitomizes the fierce Iroquois portrayed in the journals and letters of European explorers.

For nearly three weeks, the small party of Dutchmen and their Indian guides had been journeying westward along snow-covered trails through the land of the Iroquois. Among the first Europeans ever to lay eyes on this country, the Dutchmen had crossed icy rivers in bark-covered canoes, feasted on sweet pumpkins and the tangy meat of beaver and bear, slept amid dozens of clan members in smoky longhouses beneath the pelts of mountain lions and other prey, and witnessed a war game in which two teams of Mohawks in wooden armor hacked at each other with clubs and axes. Yet nothing they had observed along the way impressed them more than the sight that confronted them now. Ahead on a hilltop stood the main village of the Oneida Nation, girded by a double palisade. This "castle," as the Dutch referred to such Iroquois fortresses, bore unmistakable signs that the inhabitants were not to be trifled with: Atop the entrance stood three carved wooden men, adorned with scalps taken in battle. To reach the stronghold, the visitors had to pass between two rows of villagers, who stood respectfully in ranks to welcome them now but who had formed similar reception lines on earlier occasions to beat and berate enemy prisoners.

The travelers who walked this friendly gantlet were led by Harmen van den Bogaert, a 23-year-old barber-surgeon at the Dutch trading post of Fort Orange, located on the Hudson River near present-day Albany. His party, consisting of two other Dutchmen and five Mohawk guides, had left Fort Orange on December 11, 1634, to investigate the cause of a recent decline in the number of furs brought to the fort by the Iroquois. Unaware that a smallpox epidemic among the Indians was disrupting trade, the Dutch were inclined to blame French competition and hoped that Bogaert could induce the Mohawk and their western neighbors, the Oneida, to spurn other offers and frequent Fort Orange as they had in the past. The Dutch were particularly worried by reports of French activity in Oneida country, and thus Bogaert's visit there took on special importance.

His mission to the Oneida began badly. Soon after his party entered the fortified village on December 30, an Oneida chief approached Bogaert

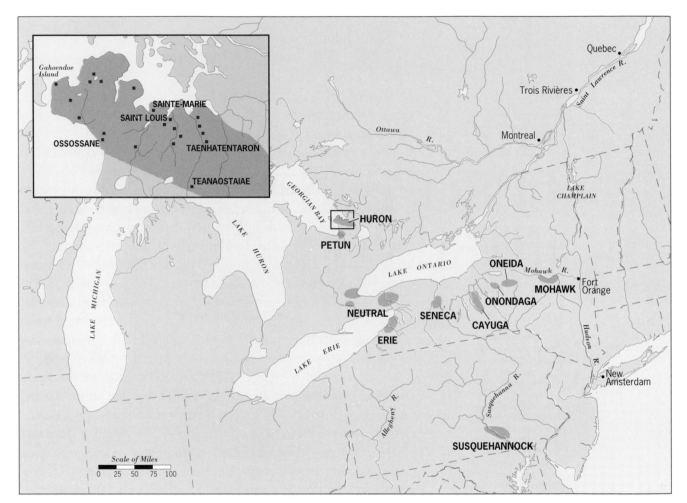

By the late 1640s, ancient rivalries fueled
by the competition for trade goods and furs
set the stage for the so-called Beaver Wars.
This map shows tribal territories and cen-
ters of European settlement just prior to the
time that the Five Nations struck out
against their Iroquoian neighbors, launch-
ing a devastating series of attacks on the
villages of Huron country (inset).

and asked what the Dutchmen were doing in his country and what they
brought for gifts. "I said that we brought him nothing," Bogaert wrote,
"but that we just came for a visit." In fact, Bogaert had offered gifts to
helpful Mohawks earlier in the journey, and he had more presents in reserve, but he wanted clear signs of cooperation from the Oneida before
he parted with any. To the Oneida, this was no way for friends to behave.
Speaking through a Mohawk interpreter, the chief made it clear to these
Dutch "scoundrels," as he called them, that guests who offered nothing
"were worth nothing." French traders, he added pointedly, had recently
offered the Oneida handsome gifts when they came seeking beaver furs.

The following day, tension between the visitors and their hosts eased
somewhat when the village headman, Arenias, returned from a peacemaking mission to neighboring Indians bearing belts of wampum he had

received to seal the accord. To honor Arenias and celebrate New Year's Eve, the Dutchmen fired their pistols three times, delighting the Indians, who knew little of firearms and were fascinated by the noise and smoke.

On New Year's Day, however, the Oneida and the Dutch again locked horns at a council meeting attended by 40 or 50 villagers. Again an Oneida spokesman berated the visitors as scoundrels, using such harsh tones that tears sprang to the eyes of one of Bogaert's companions. At that, the spokesman seemed surprised and asked why the visitors were so upset. Bogaert tossed the Indian's barb back at him, calling him a scoundrel, only to be met with laughter and words of conciliation. "You must not be angry," the spokesman insisted. "We are happy that you have come here." In characteristic Iroquois fashion, he had expressed himself freely and forcefully, but he would not allow ill feelings to disrupt the unity of the council circle, to which the Dutch had been freely admitted. Reassured, Bogaert was at last forthcoming with presents—knives, scissors, awls, and needles—handy implements much sought after by the Indians.

This exchange set the stage for trade talks between the two sides. Before discussing terms, however, the Oneida wanted to be sure that their guests trusted them—a prerequisite for good trading relations among the Iroquois. On January 3, Bogaert reported, several Oneida elders approached the Dutchmen "and said that they wanted to be our friends, and that we must not be afraid." One Indian placed his hand over Bogaert's heart to see if it was racing with fear. Satisfied that his spirit was at ease, the elders presented Bogaert and his companions with a beaver coat. "It is for your journey," they explained solicitously, "because you are so tired." The Oneidas went on to point out that their people, too, were required to make a long and taxing journey to bring furs to Fort Orange and that it pained them to come away with little in return. They then spelled out what they expected to receive in exchange for each beaver pelt they brought to market—four hands of wampum and four hands of rough wool cloth. Bogaert promised to refer their terms to his superiors and return with a response in the spring. "You must not lie," the Oneidas told him. "Come in the spring to us and bring us all an answer. If we receive four hands, then we shall trade our pelts with no one else."

Although Bogaert would not return as promised, other Dutch officials would visit Iroquois country in the years to come in the hope of monopolizing trade with the energetic People of the Longhouse. For their part, the Iroquois would continue to welcome Dutchmen bearing gifts and seek concessions from them. As Bogaert's dealings with the Oneida made clear, the Iroquois were not reluctant partners in this courtship. To the contrary, they often led the way, seeking an accord that would bring them a regular supply of trade goods.

They could hardly do otherwise, because trade with the Europeans was becoming an imperative for the inhabitants of Iroquoia. For more than a century, barter between white men and Indians had been altering lifestyles in the northern woodlands, benefiting some tribes at the expense of others, increasing the dependence of native groups on European wares, and exposing indigenous peoples to deadly diseases whose ravages made it all the more difficult for the survivors to preserve their traditional patterns of subsistence.

Fishermen and explorers from various European ports had initiated this fateful interchange along the Northeast coast in the late 1400s. By 1600 permanent trading posts had been established inland by the French, who ventured up the Saint Lawrence and later probed westward into Huron country, seeking beaver pelts for the broad-brimmed felt hats then fashionable in Europe. These forays increased hostilities between the favored trading partners of the French—including Algonquian-speaking tribes and the Iroquoian-speaking Huron—and the envious Five Nations Iroquois, who coveted the wares their northern rivals were receiving for their pelts, including metal tools and weapons that greatly enhanced the efforts of artisans and warriors. Thus when Dutch traders appeared along the Hudson in the early 1600s offering similar prizes for beaver pelts, the Mohawk and their league partners to the west saw an opportunity to even the score with their native foes.

That relations with white men could also bring sorrows would only gradually become apparent to the Iroquois. For now, they were intent on securing the fruits of European trade, which conferred both material benefits and intangible rewards in terms of honor and prestige. The Dutch, for example, offered Indians who brought them beaver pelts not only metal and cloth but strings of wampum. But to acquire such tokens of esteem from the Dutch at Fort Orange, the Mohawk first had to contend with the Algonquian-speaking Mahican, whose ancestral territory included a sliver of land between Mohawk country and the fort. For a time, the Mahican permitted Mohawks bound for Fort Orange to cross their land unharmed, and the Mohawk returned the favor, allowing the Mahican access to hunting grounds to the west. But tensions surfaced, and in 1624 fighting broke out. So intent were Mohawk chiefs on prevailing that they interrupted hostilities with their Algonquian rivals trading with the French to the north and sent all their war parties against the Mahican.

The Dutch remained loyal to the beleaguered Mahican for a time, but they paid a price. During one battle, Mohawks seized a Dutch colonist who had joined a Mahican war party. After setting fire to his body, they chopped off his arms and legs and carried them back to camp. By 1628 the relentless Mohawk had driven the Mahican away from Fort Orange and locked up trade with the Dutch.

Bitter feelings lingered between the masters of Fort Orange and their assertive new trading partners. Dutch freebooters sometimes assailed Mohawk bands in the woods and seized their furs or held chiefs for ransom. Eventually, the abuses became so flagrant that some Mohawks drew on their native tradition of appealing grievances to councils and complained to Dutch magistrates. One chief asked the magistrates to "forbid the Dutch to molest the Indians as heretofore by kicking, beating, and assaulting them." The judges assented, ordering Dutch traders not to abuse the native peoples or "take away their beavers by force." Although such legal concessions were rare, the diplomatic efforts of Bogaert and later emissaries helped ease tensions and maintain the traffic in furs between the Iroquois and the Dutch.

No amount of goodwill, however, could avert the effects of the overhunting of beaver by the Mohawk and their Iroquois allies. "I cannot get over my surprise as to the changes which are said to have occurred in the fur trade at Fort Orange," wrote a Dutch merchant in 1640. "The trouble is not with the price of the skins but with the quantity." In addition, the thick pelts the Europeans coveted came from beaver inhabiting colder climes to the north and west of the Five Nations. Thus, to maintain trade with the Dutch, the Iroquois increasingly had to serve as middlemen, obtaining prime pelts from rival groups by force if necessary.

The conflicts that ensued would be known to Europeans as the Beaver Wars, but the Iroquois did not see them that way. Culling booty in the form of furs was simply an added incentive for warriors who were driven by the age-old need to prove their courage and seek recompense. The emergence of the Great League of Peace meant that young men who nursed ambitions or grievances could no longer lash out at their fellow Iroquois. Yet the yearning for retribution remained strong, particularly in times of mourning, when warriors were expected to allay the bitterness and grief of their kin by attacking their foes and claiming prisoners.

As it happened, increased contact with Europeans in the 17th century

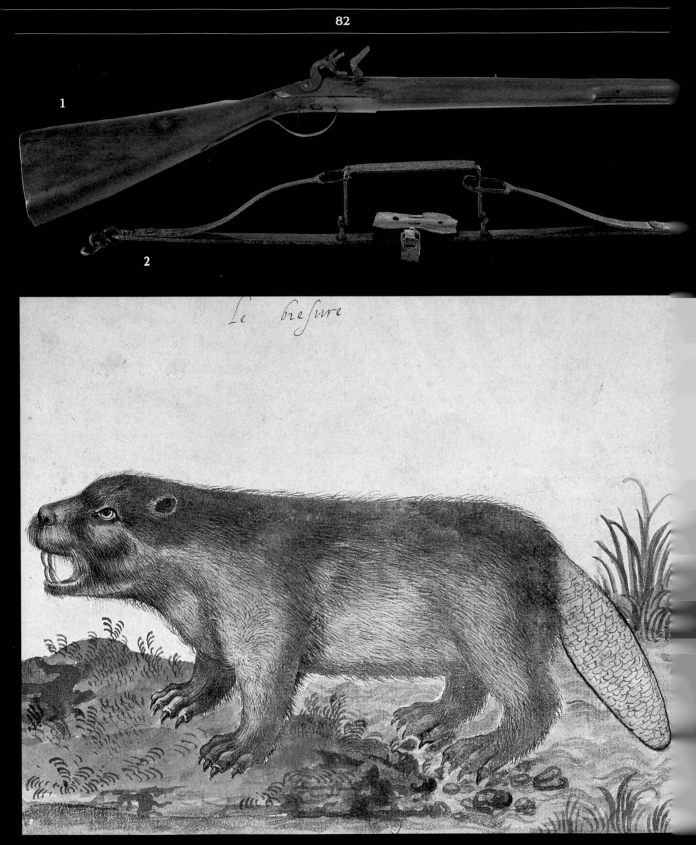

Le biesure

Looking more like predator than prey, the New World beaver in this 16th-century French watercolor reflects the common European conception of rodents as aggressive despoilers. In actuality, beavers were slaughtered in droves for their precious pelts—in 1633 alone, the Iroquois delivered nearly 30,000 skins to the traders of New Netherland.

AN APPETITE FOR TRADE

Like other Indians, the Iroquois were quick to take advantage of the white man's tools and weapons. Their appetite for such goods was first whetted in the late 1500s with knives and axes taken in raids on tribes who had traded with the French.

Within a few decades, the trading proliferated. On his journey through Iroquois country late in 1634, the Dutchman Harmen van den Bogaert noted that his Indian hosts had "good timber axes, French shirts, coats, and razors." And in many of the long-

houses, piles of beaver skins lay waiting for the spring trading season.

The beaver, whose pelt was prized for making European gentlemen's hats, became a prime commodity that the Iroquois exchanged for a wealth of goods. Although beaver was only a mi-

nor resource in their economy before the arrival of the whites, the Iroquois easily adjusted to the new demand.

Hunters would set out in the early winter when the animals bore their thickest coats and their tracks could be easily followed in the snow. After a month or two, they would return, as Dutch chronicler Adriaen Van der Donck related in 1656, "with from 40 to 80 beaver skins, and with some otter, fishers, and other skins also." Over the next months, the skins were cleaned and preserved.

The pelts were often worn for a time, since a little wear, bear grease, and sweat softened the fur, thereby increasing its value to hat makers.

The furs were brought to market at European outposts between May and November. There, merchants bartered with

trappers for the beaver pelts, and the Indians returned home laden with knives, axes, hoes, cooking pots, needles, scissors, awls, nails, and woolen cloth, all of which gradually became part of Iroquois life. For a time, the colonists strove to keep firearms out of Indian hands, but by the 1640s, guns were just another commodity, and the prize possessions of hundreds of warriors.

At first, the foreign goods simply eased the Indians' labors and even spawned new hybrid crafts; brass pots, for example, were carved into dozens of ornamental and practical items. But by the mid-17th century, the Iroquois had become dependent on European wares. Many traditional tools and materials fell into disuse, and native artisans applied most of their skill to the decorative and ceremonial arts.

1 This flintlock is of the type produced by the Dutch for sale to the Iroquois in the mid-1600s.
2 Iron beaver traps, like this English model dating from the 1740s, were much sought after by Iroquois hunters.
3 With a bone handle and sloped blade tip, the so-called Flemish knife was traded widely in New York and Pennsylvania.
4, 5 Producing sparks when struck with flint, firesteels were the matches of their day and highly prized by the Iroquois.
6 Rugged brass pots—this one came from a village destroyed in 1687—all but replaced clay vessels in a few decades.

occasioned widespread mourning among the Iroquois. Waves of alien diseases swept over their lands in the 1630s, killing thousands of Mohawks, Oneidas, Cayugas, Onondagas, and Senecas. Reports from the region catalog epidemic after epidemic, from "a general malady among the Mohawk" one year, to "a great mortality among the Onondaga" another year. By the 1640s, the population of the Five Nations had been cut from more than 20,000 at the time of first contact to roughly 10,000.

On a practical level, these losses disrupted the native economy and made the goods the Iroquois obtained in exchange for furs all the more important. But in personal terms, the surviving Iroquois warriors were primarily concerned with compensating for the deaths and restoring the strength of their people. To that end, they sought enemy captives, some for torture but increasing numbers for adoption to replace loved ones who had died. If, in the process, Iroquois warriors could seize valuable furs and trade goods from their foes, so much the better.

The determination of the Iroquois to recoup their losses through battle spelled trouble for the Huron in particular. There had long been bad blood between the Huron and the westernmost Iroquois, the Seneca. Almost every year, warriors from one side or the other would paddle their canoes along the shores of Lake Ontario, bound for enemy territory, where they would take prisoners and carry off booty. The arrival of Europeans aggravated this old feud. In the early 1600s, for example, the French explorer Champlain and his musketeers joined the Huron in attacks on the Iroquois that handed the Seneca and their league partners punishing lessons in European tactics.

Iroquois hostility toward the Huron was further fueled by the advantages those allies of the French enjoyed in the fur trade. Both the Iroquois and Huron reaped large harvests of corn and other crops, but the Huron were better positioned to exchange their surplus with nearby tribes who subsisted mainly as hunter-gatherers and periodically had need of food. In return, those tribes provided the Huron with pelts, including prime beaver furs, which the Huron then offered to the French for their wares. But to preserve ties with the French, the Huron had to accept Jesuit missionaries, whose presence subjected Huron society to stresses that the Iroquois had yet to experience. Through their fervent preachings, the Black Robes, as Indians termed the Jesuits, divided the Huron into two camps—those who welcomed the priests and embraced their God, and those who rejected the new faith and its followers as agents of evil and pestilence.

The Jesuit campaign in Huron country began in earnest in 1634 when

Assisted by their Huron and Algonquian allies, French soldiers under the command of Samuel de Champlain attack a palisaded Iroquois village—portrayed here inaccurately in the neat geometric form characteristic of European forts of that period. The assault, which occurred in 1615, was one of several launched against the Iroquois by Champlain in his effort to show his support for the Huron and Algonquian peoples.

the indefatigable Father Jean de Brébeuf established a mission at the village of Ihonatiria, on Georgian Bay. With Huron labor, Father Brébeuf built a longhouse in the village where he and his colleagues could live and work. This enabled the Black Robes to minister to the villagers at close quarters without experiencing the presumed indecencies of life in the Hurons' crowded dwellings. The Jesuits were so shy of physical exposure that when traveling from village to village with Huron guides, they would not undress in their presence even to bathe. As one missionary put it, sharing a longhouse with the Huron was out of the question, for "religious eyes could not endure the sight of so much lewdness."

Residents of Ihonatiria were less inhibited about entering the longhouse of the Black Robes, where they were charmed by various intriguing gadgets Father Brébeuf had cleverly installed—magnifying glasses, a clock, even a mill for grinding flour. These devices, many Hurons felt, were signs of the Jesuits' supernatural powers. The noises the clock made were thought to emanate from a spirit, for example, and Hurons dubbed the device "headman of the day."

Nonetheless, many Hurons remained skeptical about Christianity itself. The principles Father Brébeuf and his colleagues espoused to the villagers as they mastered their language clashed with cherished Huron values. The villagers believed, for example, that little children should never be scolded or hit, that youngsters past puberty should be free to consort sexually with their opposites, and that a husband and wife who no longer cared for each other should be allowed to separate. All this was anathema to the Jesuits, and their efforts to instill Catholic morality in converts often stirred up trouble. Young women who heeded the priests and held themselves apart from eager young men before marriage, for example, were looked upon by Huron traditionalists as unnatural and ungenerous. Indeed, such aloof behavior was often associated with witches. So strong was the attachment of some Hurons to communal traditions that when they were told by priests that they would go to heaven if they accepted baptism while their neighbors who declined would go to hell, they refused the sacrament on the grounds that the souls of all the villagers must reside in one place together.

Wearing armor made from sticks laced together with sinew, a Huron warrior clutches a hatchet and a bow. Such armor, worn during ritualized head-to-head clashes, fell out of favor soon after the introduction of firearms.

Despite such obstacles, Father Brébeuf and his colleagues continued to draw converts through patient instruction, combined with calculated appeals to native beliefs and superstitions. The priests often began their services by dispensing tobacco, which had sacred associations for the Indians. And when drought struck in the spring of 1635, Father Brébeuf agreed to appeal for rain if the people would change their ways. After a Huron shaman failed to summon storms with traditional ceremonies, the priests led a procession of the faithful through Ihonatiria. As they marched, showers descended and persisted for some time, and the Black Robes gained stature in the community.

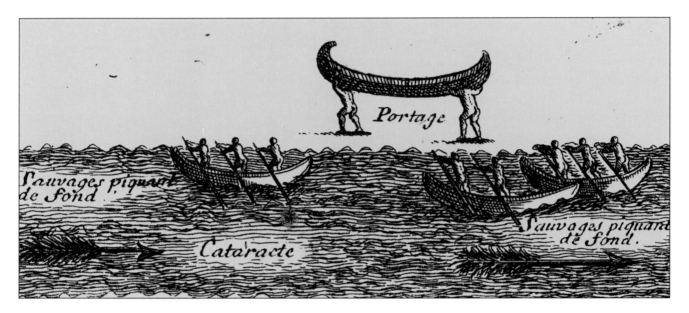

Portage

Sauvages piquant de fond

Cataracte

Sauvages piquant de fond.

A French engraving depicts two Iroquois warriors portaging their bark canoe while others pole their craft through rapids. The Iroquois were master boatmen who traveled by river and lake whenever possible.

The Huron were more uneasy about the power the priests seemed to wield over disease. Frequently, the Jesuits baptized Hurons who were very ill to save their souls from the torments of hell. Many of those baptized perished, but others rallied, and disputes raged among the Huron as to whether baptism caused or cured deadly afflictions. Soon the epidemics worsened, and more than a few Hurons denounced the Jesuits as witches who were weaving destructive spells. As proof of Jesuit sorcery, the Huron pointed to the priests' custom of closing their doors to the Huron at certain times of the day—reclusive behavior that was intrinsically suspicious to people who spent almost all their time in the company of others. Other Hurons reported dreams that linked the Black Robes with the spread of disease. In one such vision, the dreamer told of watching a Jesuit open a book that unleashed hundreds of tiny flames spreading pestilence. Even some Jesuits suspected a link between their missionary activities and disease. "These barbarians have apparent reasons for thus reproaching us," wrote one priest, "inasmuch as the scourges which humble the proud precede us or accompany us wherever we go."

As suspicions increased, the lives of Jesuits were threatened, and Father Brébeuf himself suffered a brutal beating. In the end, however, the Black Robes were spared; the Huron had become too dependent on European goods to risk alienating the priests. One headman warned that expulsion of the Jesuits—and the resultant loss of the fur trade—would make beggars of the Huron. Meeting with Huron leaders in Quebec in

1635, Champlain demanded that the priests be respected if the Huron wished to continue trading along the Saint Lawrence River. Christian Indians received more for their furs, and in one instance in 1640, several Huron traders who spoke out against the Jesuits were imprisoned in Quebec. Heeding these lessons, local chiefs reconciled themselves to the presence of the priests, and new missions sprouted up. But beneath the surface, traditionalists continued to resent the Black Robes and their native followers. Thus the Huron found themselves at odds even as the Iroquois closed ranks against them.

As their conflict with the Huron escalated in the 1640s, the Iroquois profited both by their warrior heritage and by the new weapons supplied by their white trading partners. The Dutch, who had little interest in converting the Iroquois and dealt with them mainly at secure trading posts, overcame their initial reluctance and sold the Iroquois muskets for use against their rivals in the fur trade. By contrast, the French feared for their missionaries in Huron country and restricted the sale of guns to the most loyal converts. This made it more difficult for the Huron to cope with Iroquois war parties that were assailing them from all directions in all seasons.

Traditionally, rival Iroquoians had confined their fighting to the times when the leaves were on the trees. But now the Huron faced attack year round. Well-armed Iroquois—mostly Mohawks and Oneidas—repeatedly hit trading parties traveling the Saint Lawrence. No sooner did one war band return home than another replaced it. In 1643 a group of 40 Mohawks ambushed a flotilla of Huron canoes near Montreal. Twenty-three Hurons were captured; 13 were beaten to death and 10 were carried off. The Mohawks netted so many furs that they were unable to bring them all home.

While the eastern Iroquois prowled the trade routes, the Onondaga and Cayuga joined the Seneca in infiltrating Huron territory, where they lurked in the forests and descended on fields and hamlets to claim enemy lives and pilfer furs and other goods. The Huron dispatched war parties to retaliate, but they met with limited success. On one occasion, a band of 100 Hurons was surrounded by an Iroquois force

The artfully crafted Iroquois war clubs shown here and on the following pages—including one built tomahawk-style with a metal blade in place of a wooden ball (right)—proved as lethal as they were lovely. The French called them cassetêtes, or "head breakers."

several times that size and routed; not a single Huron escaped capture or death—a frightful toll at a time when the loss of more than a few warriors was cause for concern. Some of the Iroquois attacks in Huron country seemed to be designed purely to demoralize the populace. A small group of people gathering hemp were set upon at night and slain; a group of women working in a field were whisked away so quickly they could not be rescued. Huron women became too scared to till and plant, and villages were soon short of food.

Pressure on the Huron eased in 1645 when Mohawk chiefs responded to peace overtures from the alarmed French. The negotiations, which drew some 400 Indians, including Hurons and their Algonquian allies, took place at the French settlement of Trois Rivières, between Montreal and Quebec. Delegates traded gifts and lofty speeches, but the pact that emerged was tenuous. According to its terms, the Mohawk and the Huron were to exchange captives, and the Mohawk were granted access to northern hunting grounds and allowed to trade with the French and their Indian allies. Yet hunting and trading yielded the Mohawk fewer furs than their raids had. And warriors on both sides looked forward to resuming the forays that brought them prestige and satisfied the enduring thirst for vengeance. Any lingering French hopes for a lasting accord dissolved in September 1646, when a Jesuit who had been captured by Mohawks and then released returned in peace to the village where he had been held, only to be executed as a witch for causing plague and pestilence.

Soon the Mohawk and their Iroquois allies were again targeting the Huron, only this time the war parties were even larger and their aims more ambitious. In a campaign without precedent, Iroquois chiefs combined forces to raze entire Huron settlements. Just how this effort was conceived and coordinated remains a mystery, but the end result was nothing less than the destruction of the Huron as an independent people. Some Hurons anticipated disaster and tried to avert it. In the spring of 1648, a small group of traditionalists rose up against the Jesuits with the apparent aim of breaking ties with the French and coming to terms with the Iroquois. But the abortive revolt did little more than underscore the dissension within Huron ranks.

A few months later, hundreds of Senecas well stocked with Dutch muskets infiltrated Huron country and set their sights on the village of Teanaostaiae, one of the largest and best-fortified Huron settlements. At daybreak on July 4, the warriors burst into the village and rained fire upon the startled residents, many of whom were leaving church after a sunrise

mass. Following this deadly volley, Senecas swept through the town, looting longhouses and putting them to the torch. The presiding priest, Father Antoine Daniel, encouraged the Hurons to fight, but the attackers could not be contained. Finally, the Senecas stormed the church, where many Hurons had taken refuge. Father Daniel stood at the front door to divert the enemy while Hurons slipped out the back. The priest was soon cut down by musket fire and arrows. Iroquois then stripped off his robes, cut his body in pieces, and flung the parts into the church, which by now was ablaze. The toll of Hurons killed or captured—700 out of a village of 2,000—was devastating. One-tenth of the entire Huron population had been wiped out at once. The smoldering village was abandoned forever.

This day of Iroquois rage accomplished more for Christianity among the Huron than years of missionary activity. Traditionalists renounced any remaining notion that breaking with the French would appease the Iroquois, and the Jesuits recorded many new converts. Thousands of Hurons visited the Jesuit headquarters of Sainte-Marie, seeking food and shelter. At the mission town of Ossossane, chiefs appointed the local priest headman and empowered him to forbid traditional ritual. When an ailing man later asked that friends of his conduct a curing rite involving sexual intercourse, his wish was denied—a notable departure from the ancient custom of indulging the desires of the sick. About the same time, some married couples began resorting to prayer to settle disputes that might otherwise have led them to separate, and at least one mother defied tradition by striking her unruly child. In March 1649, eight months after the Iroquois attack on Teanaostaiae, the head of the Huron missions wrote to his superior in Rome: "Such is the condition of this house, and indeed of the whole mission, that I think hardly anything could be added to the piety, obedience, humility, patience, and charity of our brethren."

Piety alone could not restore the fighting strength of the Huron, however. Just weeks after that sanguine letter was written, the Iroquois struck again. Over the winter, a combined force of more than 1,000 Seneca and Mohawk warriors had camped undetected in the forests on the north shore of Lake Ontario, below the main Huron settlements. Now, on the night of March 16, with snow still blanketing the ground, they approached the village of Taenhatentaron. Fortifications there had recently been strengthened by the French and were thought to be impregnable, but many of the inhabitants had left, seeking refuge elsewhere, and the rest were not expecting an attack in winter. Creeping up in the darkness, the Iroquois opened a breach in the walls and poured through before

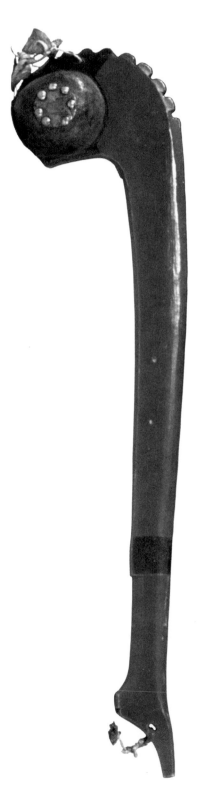

most of the Hurons could rouse themselves from sleep. The attackers took the town easily, losing only 10 of their own men and allowing few of the 400 or so Hurons to escape. Part of the Iroquois force broke off and headed for the mission village of Saint Louis, three miles away. Hurons fleeing the first attack arrived there first, however, and most of the villagers got away, leaving the sick and elderly behind with 80 determined Huron warriors and two tenacious Jesuits: Father Gabriel Lalemant and the pioneering Father Brébeuf.

The outnumbered defenders of Saint Louis fended off two assaults before the Iroquois smashed the palisades and entered the village. The old and sick were killed outright; the warriors were either slain in battle or taken captive. After torching the village, the attackers returned to Taenhatentaron with their prisoners, among them Fathers Brébeuf and Lalemant. Observers at the headquarters of Sainte-Marie, three miles to the northwest, watched with alarm as flames shot into the sky.

The two captive Jesuits were tortured in traditional fashion. As soon as they were taken, their nails were ripped from their fingers and they were stripped of their clothing. Upon reaching Taenhatentaron, they were forced to walk a gantlet of warriors, who beat them mercilessly and bound them to wooden stakes. Father Lalemant lingered on in agony until the following morning, but Father Brébeuf's ordeal was even more intense, and he died that same day. At one point, his tormentors fashioned a band of red-hot metal hatchets and hung it over his neck; later they tied a bark belt, filled with pitch and resin, around his waist and set it afire. Among the torturers were Hurons who had been captured and adopted by the Iroquois and now regarded the priests as enemies. In a mockery of Christian rite, one of them scalded Father Brébeuf three times with boiling water and pronounced: "Go to heaven, for thou art well baptized." Through all this, Father Brébeuf maintained a stoicism worthy of the bravest of his opponents. He continued to preach to his tormentors, so infuriating them that they cut out his tongue and slashed his lips. Finally, they scalped the priest and pierced his chest. Warriors impressed with his courage ate his heart, while others drank his blood.

The next day, the Iroquois marched toward Sainte-Marie, hoping to complete their triumph—and claim more furs and prisoners for use in bargaining with the French. But the Hurons at Sainte-Marie held their ground. They drove an advance party of Iroquois warriors back to Saint Louis and retook the village. When the main body of Iroquois arrived shortly thereafter, a furious battle erupted and raged past sunset. In the end, the Iroquois prevailed, slaughtering all but about 20 Hurons, but losing nearly 100 of their own men in the process. Sobered by the toll, the main Iroquois force turned homeward several days later, killing those captives who could not keep up and burdening the rest with booty.

Word of the latest Iroquois attacks sparked a wholesale abandonment of the remaining Huron villages. Many of the exiles fled to Gahoendoe Island in Georgian Bay, some 30 miles north of Sainte-Marie. There the entire Jesuit mission joined them and helped clear fields and plant crops. Over the summer, Gahoendoe's population swelled to several thousand—far more than could be supported by the scant acreage the newcomers had been able to cultivate. The community supplemented its crops with fish and wild plants, but even then small groups were obliged to forage for food on the mainland, where bands of Iroquois warriors still roved, picking off Huron remnants. By winter, disease and malnutrition had set in, and the refugees were scrabbling for bits of bark and fungus. In a bid to conserve food, the Jesuits allotted the Indians small copper tokens, to be exchanged for acorns, fish, and cornmeal gruel. Each noon, Hurons who had once raised enough bounty to feed neighboring tribes assembled outside the stone fort occupied by the Jesuits to receive their meager rations. Perhaps 600 Gahoendoe Hurons survived the winter. Half of those left for Quebec the following summer accompanied by the Jesuits; less than a year later, the last group of Indians departed the island. By the summer of 1651, Huron country was virtually uninhabited.

Those refugees who did not flee to the island colony sought haven with friendly Iroquoian-speaking groups in the region—including the Petun, the Neutral, and the Erie. But there were few safe harbors for the Huron in this storm. Buoyed by the swift collapse of Huron resistance, Iroquois war parties soon lashed out at the groups who were sheltering the survivors. The prime motive behind these attacks, apparently, was to prevent the Huron from regrouping, but there were furs to be taken as well, and the Iroquois may also have hoped to take control of the beaver trade and dictate terms to the French. Once again, chiefs of the Five Nations mustered large forces and attacked mercilessly. The Petun and the Neutral were dispersed by the autumn of 1651; a small number of Hurons among the Petun escaped capture and fled west, where they became known as the Wyandot. The main Erie community succumbed in 1654, although bands of Eries resisted for a few more years.

Iroquois warriors gained prestige and booty from these forays, but the chief result for the Five Nations was thousands of captives, most of

Taken prisoner by the Iroquois on March 16, 1649, Jesuit Fathers Jean de Brébeuf and Gabriel Lalemant endure various cruelties inflicted by their captors. One tormentor pours boiling water on Brébeuf, who died the day he was captured. Lalemant clung to life until the next morning.

whom were adopted to compensate for losses caused by disease and war. In one instance, a band of more than 500 Huron refugees was incorporated wholesale into the Seneca Nation, where they started a village of their own. Such newcomers replenished the Iroquois population, but they also included a number of Christian converts whose presence made Iroquois society more complex and contentious. In effect, the Huron bequeathed their divided heritage to the Iroquois. As one Huron explained to a Mohawk war party with whom he pleaded for refuge: "I am going to my country, to seek out my relatives and friends. The country of the Hurons is no longer where it was—you have transported it into your own."

Even as Iroquois warriors acted together to disperse rival groups, discord was brewing among the chiefs of the Five Nations. At one point, the Mohawk sought support from the Seneca for a proposed attack on the French at Montreal and Trois Rivières, but the Seneca balked, claiming that they needed all their strength to deal with the Erie. In fact, the Seneca—like the other Iroquois to the west of the Mohawk—nurtured a grudge against their easternmost brothers. As the nation closest to the Dutch, the Mohawk had garnered the most in weapons and other trade goods. And their league partners were beholden to them for access to Fort Orange. In declining to lend support to the proposed attack, Seneca chiefs, backed by like-minded leaders of the other western nations, hoped to cut the Mohawk down to size and keep alive the possibility of reaching an understanding with the French that would end their annoying dependence on the distant Dutch.

The French, stung by the dispersal of the Huron, were eager to pursue this opening, and in 1653 they reached an accord with the four western nations. Onondaga chiefs were particularly ingratiating, inviting the French to settle on their lands and help defend their villages against enemy attack. Alarmed by such maneuvers, the Mohawk patched together their own truce with the French that same year.

Like the Huron before them, the Iroquois recognized that the French favored those who embraced their missionaries. To that end, the Mohawk and Onondaga competed to have a French mission placed on their soil. The French were inclined to trust in the Onondaga, and when the Mohawk learned of their plans, they sent a delegation to Quebec in 1654 to try to dissuade them. The Mohawk spokesman, Chief Canaqueese, argued his case using the metaphor of the longhouse, of which the Mohawk

A painting by Frederic Remington depicts an amicable exchange between Indians and Frenchmen on a street in 17th-century Montreal. Many members of Great Lakes tribes befriended French traders and embraced Catholicism—a partnership that stirred up jealousy and suspicion among the Iroquois.

were Keepers of the Eastern Door and the Onondaga Keepers of the Central Fire. "Ought not one to enter a house by the door," he asked, "and not by the chimney or roof of the cabin, unless he be a thief and wish to take the inmates by surprise? Have you no fear that the smoke may blind you, our fire not being extinguished, and that you may fall from the top to the bottom, having nothing solid on which to plant your feet?"

Despite this eloquent appeal, which hinted at trouble if the plan went ahead, the Jesuits proceeded with their mission to the Onondaga. Established in 1656, it lasted less than two years. The Jesuits found a welcome among Christian Hurons who had been adopted by the Onondaga and won a number of converts among the Iroquois population as well. But once again, epidemics shadowed their efforts. One Jesuit credited the mission with having converted "more than 500 children, and many adults, most of whom died after baptism." Such a toll might have led Onondaga traditionalists to oust the Jesuits before long, in any case, but the Mohawk hastened the mission's demise by sending warriors to attack it. Alerted by a friendly Onondaga headman named Garakontie, the priests fled with their few followers.

Undeterred by this ominous start, Jesuits soon returned to campaign for converts among the Onondaga and any western Iroquois who still hoped to placate the French and promote trade. As had happened in Hu-

Kateri Tekakwitha, a Mohawk, was baptized in 1676 at the age of 20 by Jesuits who were visiting her village of Ossernenon on the Mohawk River. Hounded by traditionalist Mohawks because of her religion, she fled to a Jesuit mission and later became the first Indian nun among the Iroquois, revered as the Lily of the Mohawks. During the second half of the 17th century, more than a few Iroquois turned away from traditional beliefs and adopted Christianity.

ron villages, rifts developed within communities; supporters of the Jesuits clashed with those who clung to the old ways. Prominent among the champions of the Black Robes was Garakontie, who used his friendship with the grateful Jesuits to increase his authority. Once baptized, he publicly rejected cherished Iroquois rituals and myths, including the ceremonies that sustained the Great League of Peace. Outraged traditionalists derided him. As one priest reported, they said that he was "no longer a man; he had become French; and since he had abandoned the customs of the country, he had also ceased to have any affection for it."

The Jesuits had some success in winning over Iroquois women, for the cult of the Virgin Mary and the female saints was consistent with the respect accorded matriarchs in Iroquois clans. More often than not, however, the missionaries' appeals fell on deaf ears. For one thing, the Iroquois prized open exchanges of opinions and did not like being preached at. One of the few Dutch ministers who proselytized the Mohawk reported ruefully that his Indian listeners would "afterward ask me what I am doing and what I want, that I stand there alone and make so many words, while none of the rest may speak." Jesuits encountered similar skepticism when they tried to play the part of a pastor leading his flock in communities where people declined to be dictated to even by their chiefs. The priests learned to their dismay that the only commands the Indians obeyed without question were those that came to them from the spirit world through dreams and other portents. Jesuits denounced such dream worship as sacrilege, but as one priest among the Onondaga conceded, dreams "seem to constitute this country's sole divinity, to which they defer in all things. They think their ruin is desired if anyone tries to do away with this divinity, which they regard as the thing that makes them live."

Nowhere was hostility to the Jesuits and to French authority in general stronger than among the Mohawk, who resented what they saw as French favoritism toward the western Iroquois and who continued to feud with the Algonquian trading partners of the French. Matters came to a head in 1665, when a seasoned French officer, Marquis Prouville de Tracy, arrived in Quebec with orders from King Louis XIV to silence hostile Iroquois by carrying war "even to their firesides in order to exterminate them." Chiefs of the four western nations avoided the sting of French bullets by pledging cooperation at Quebec and inviting the Jesuits to dispatch more missionaries. The proud Mohawk chiefs were slow to respond, however, and Tracy decided to make a lesson of them.

In the autumn of 1666, he led nearly 2,000 French troops and allied Indians into Mohawk country. The army was detected as it marched, and Mohawks fled their villages for hideouts in the forest. Tracy had their fields and settlements put to the torch, and much of the year's harvest was lost.

Hard pressed, the Mohawk bowed to French demands, which included the admission of Jesuits to their country. The priests had no illusions about converting the entire nation. Instead, they encouraged sympathetic Mohawks and the Christian converts they had adopted to move to French territory, where they would not be harassed for their beliefs. In time, several hundred Indians an-

The moccasins below are typical of those worn by the Iroquois in the 1600s. Fashioned of smoked skin and adorned with white beads, dyed porcupine quills, and metal cones, they reflect an ancient tradition of useful and decorative handiwork.

swered this call, and a large community of converts grew up along the Saint Lawrence. Named Caughnawaga, for an old village in the Mohawk River valley, the settlement drew followers from other Iroquois nations as well. For traditionalists, this was an ominous development. Foreigners had lured Iroquois away from the longhouse of the Five Nations, and it was only a matter of time before some of those who had left would be called on to take up arms against their brothers who had stayed behind.

Tracy's punishing attack on the Mohawk did nothing to reassure the western Iroquois chiefs who had been pressured into placating the French at Quebec. Indeed, growing annoyance with the French would soon restore a sense of common purpose to the league. The Five Nations were ready to be courted by a new European partner, and they were eagerly obliged by the English, who supplanted the Dutch along the Hudson in the 1660s, changing the name of Fort Orange to Albany. The western Iroquois had long regarded the Dutch as partners of the Mohawk rather

In this 18th-century sketch, the settlement of Caughnawaga sprawls along the southern bank of the Saint Lawrence opposite Montreal. Founded in 1676 by the Jesuits, the village was one of many sanctuaries for Christianized Iroquois, who were harassed by the unconverted among their own people.

Dressed in their finest outfits, a proud Mohawk family from Caughnawaga poses for a portrait at the turn of the century.

than true friends of their own, and recently even some Mohawks had begun to doubt that partnership. As one Mohawk chief put it, "The Dutch say we are brothers, and joined together with chains, but that lasts only as long as we have beavers; after that no attention is paid to us."

By contrast, the English sought an enduring relationship with the Five Nations that would help stabilize the region and provide the burgeoning crown colonies from New England to Virginia with a buffer against the French and their Indian allies. In meetings at Albany, officials of the New York Colony and chiefs of the Five Nations worked out a unique compact. Both sides used the metaphor of a silver chain to describe their covenant. Piece by piece, links were added to this chain until it joined the Five Nations with English colonies up and down the coast and with other Indian tribes of the region. The Iroquois made the covenant chain part of their mythology, surrounding it with rituals resembling those that bound the Great League of Peace. Just as all league conclaves were held in the land of the Onondaga, all gatherings of covenant chain partners took place in Albany. During those meetings, convened by the governor of New York, Iroquois orators recited the history of relations with the Dutch and the English and reaffirmed the covenant by exchanging gifts, much as they did during league ceremonies. "The covenant that is betwixt the governor general and us is inviolable," proclaimed a Mohawk chief. "If the very thunder should break upon the covenant chain, it would not break it in sunder."

Formation of the covenant chain gave the Iroquois ascendancy over Indians who had been stoutly resisting Iroquois dominance. Chief among those were the Susquehannock, the last of the Iroquoian-speaking peoples to defy the Five Nations. From their villages along the Susquehanna River in Pennsylvania, warriors bearing guns had turned the tables by raiding the Seneca and Cayuga and pilfering furs. In response, the Iroquois had mustered a large force in 1663 and marched south, where they laid siege to a strongly defended Susquehannock village. Resorting to subterfuge, the Iroquois sent a delegation of two dozen men, ostensibly to talk peace. But the Susquehannocks were not taken in. As the Iroquois passed through the palisades, they were seized, bound to scaffolds, and burned alive. The main body of Iroquois retreated, pursued for two days by the Susquehannocks.

For several years to come, the two sides traded blow for blow, with the Susquehannock more than holding their own. At one point, many Cayugas were forced to abandon their villages and flee north across Lake Ontario. In the end, however, the Susquehannock fell prey to devastating attacks from English colonists. The remnants had little choice but to accept dependence on the Iroquois, who were bolstered now by their covenant with the English. Many surviving Susquehannocks were adopted by the Iroquois in the 1670s, and once again the ranks of the Five Nations were replenished by their former enemies. Similarly,

This painting depicts a bustling woodland village, of the sort inhabited by the Ojibwa and the Cree, hugging the shore of Lake Huron. Originally denizens of the region around eastern Lake Superior and northern Lake Huron, the Ojibwa pushed southeastward, clashing with the Iroquois during the late 1600s over hunting territory and the right to trade with the Europeans.

Algonquians such as the Mahican who had remained in conflict with the Mohawk were induced by the English to become wards of the Iroquois, who referred to them thenceforth as their "children."

Although the covenant chain brought the Five Nations unaccustomed quiet along their eastern front, storm clouds were gathering to the west—much to the satisfaction of avid Iroquois warriors, who had no use for peace. As disease, strife, and the reliance on European wares had disrupted other traditional pursuits, warfare had become the consummate craft of Iroquois men. More than ever, young warriors defined their value to the community in terms of the captives and booty they could offer to their grateful kin. To satisfy such ambitions, the Iroquois needed fresh enemies, and they found them among the Algonquian-speaking peoples living around the western Great Lakes and in the woodlands stretching southward to the Ohio River. These tribes—including the Ottawa, Ojibwa, Shawnee, Miami, and Illinois—had been courted by the French as relations with the Iroquois deteriorated and were now providing Quebec with a steady supply of furs. In targeting the western Algonquians, Iroquois chiefs saw a chance to thwart the French, cull an immediate harvest of pelts, and pursue the elusive goal of controlling trade.

Raids on the western tribes often involved journeys of more than 500 miles, but Iroquois warriors could get by for months on the trail. They foraged for food along the way or, when the enemy was near, made do with the rations of cornmeal they carried. Typical of these long-distance forays was one conducted by some 500 Iroquois warriors in 1680, after a smallpox epidemic in Iroquoia increased the longing for captives and booty. Venturing into Illinois territory, the Iroquois came upon a large community whose men were away hunting and proceeded to burn huts and ransack the cemetery for grave offerings. On their way home, the marauders struck two Miami villages near Lake Michigan. After the battle, the Iroquois agreed to return all captives in exchange for 3,000 beaver pelts, a pledge they broke as soon as the pelts were handed over.

As the raids continued, the Iroquois became unruly at home as well as on the warpath. In 1682 an Onondaga war party returned from Illinois country with hundreds of prisoners. Captives were forced to run the gantlet as usual, but the villagers were not content with blows and insults—they attacked the prisoners with such fury that many might have died if Onondaga chiefs had not intervened. Later, captives were again assaulted by a band of drunks who burst into a longhouse where some Illinois were being sheltered. As a Jesuit priest who witnessed the debacle wrote,

THE ART OF THE COMB

An ancient form of ornamentation, carved hair combs are testimony to the skill and imagination of Iroquois artisans. The combs were worn by men, women, and children and came in a wide array of sculpted designs. The earliest combs long predate the arrival of the Europeans. Carved from wood, bone, or antler, they were simple and sturdy, with three to five thick teeth, and often featured animal figures. Beginning in the late 16th century, when metal tools were readily available to the Iroquois, comb making flourished, and the complexity and variety of designs expanded almost without limit.

Armed now with implements that enabled them to carve with much greater precision, Iroquois—and especially Seneca—artisans gave free rein to their creative spirit. These combs, which were now made with as many as 25 teeth, were crowned with a fantastic array of animal and human figures, supernatural and legendary effigies, and symbolic imagery. Frequently rendered in symmetrical pairs symbolizing the harmonic balance of the natural world, the designs reflect the rich spiritual universe of the Iroquois.

A delicately carved Seneca comb portrays the three Elder Brothers of the Iroquois League—Seneca, Onondaga, and Mohawk—sitting hand in hand beneath two wolves. Like other animals depicted on such combs, the wolves may be clan symbols.

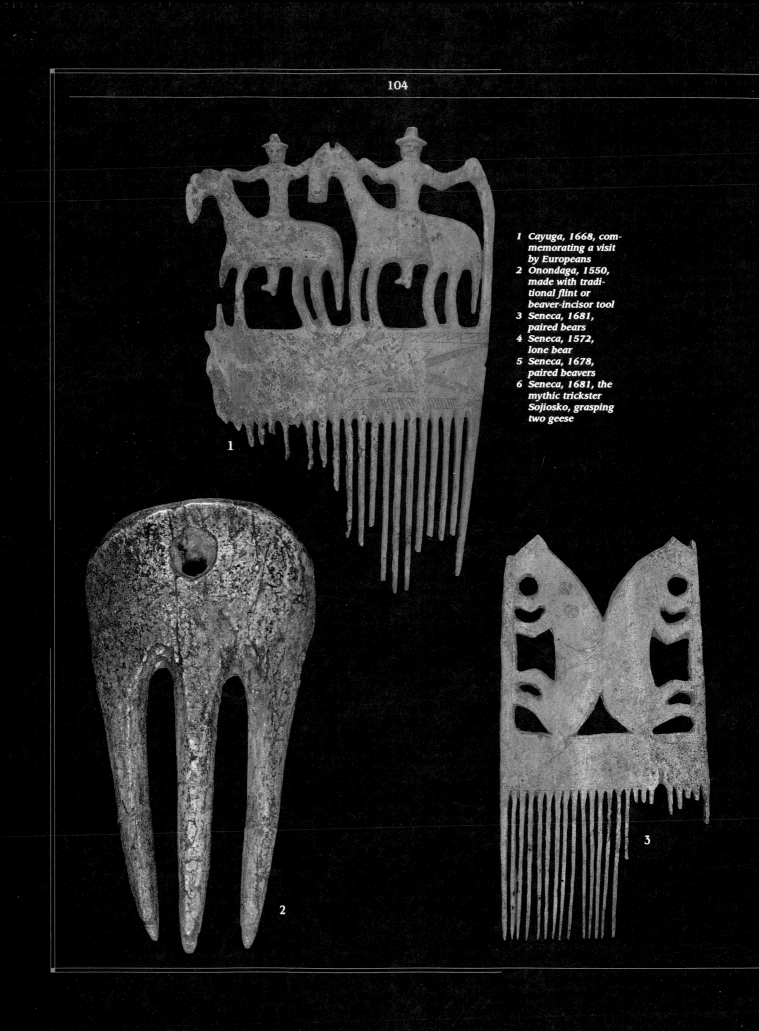

1 Cayuga, 1668, commemorating a visit by Europeans
2 Onondaga, 1550, made with traditional flint or beaver-incisor tool
3 Seneca, 1681, paired bears
4 Seneca, 1572, lone bear
5 Seneca, 1678, paired beavers
6 Seneca, 1681, the mythic trickster Sojiosko, grasping two geese

4

5

6

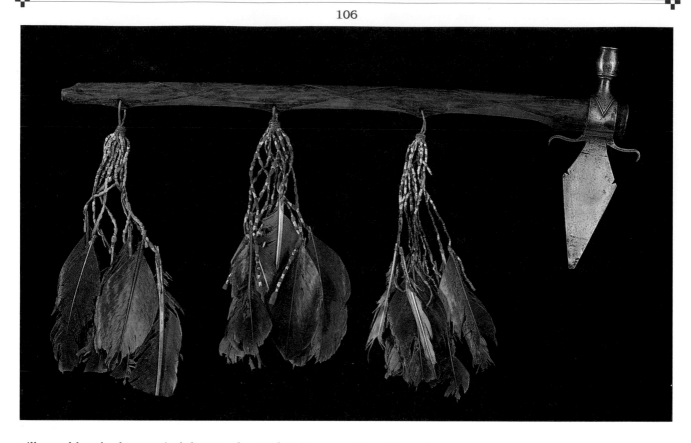

village elders had to remind the attackers "that it was contrary to custom to ill-treat prisoners" before their fate had been decided.

Evidently, time-honored Iroquois traditions were crumbling under the stress of chronic warfare, disease, and the difficulty of absorbing vast numbers of newcomers, whose adoption saddled the Five Nations with unforeseen obligations. The Susquehannock, for example, had acquired many enemies in Pennsylvania and the south before their exodus, and they endowed those animosities to the Iroquois when they joined them. Soon tribes in Virginia and the Carolinas had been added to the long list of Iroquois foes. Whether they lay to the south or to the west, few of these opponents were easily subdued. Iroquois warriors were spending more time away from their homes, with less to show for it when they returned.

Aware that the Iroquois were overextended and eager to punish them for harrying their trade routes, the French prepared to attack the Five Nations. As war loomed in 1686, Iroquois chiefs nervously looked to the English for promises of assistance. New York governor Thomas Dongan, who wanted the French bloodied at no expense to the English, addressed the chiefs condescendingly as "my children" and "subjects to the king of England" and offered them vague assurances. "When I see that the French start the war," he proclaimed, "you will see what I will do." In fact, when push came to shove, English forces would challenge the French only where prized colonial possessions were at stake. Otherwise, the English were content to let the Iroquois bear the brunt of the fighting.

The French aimed their first blows at the Keepers of the Western

Its steel bowl and blade made this ceremonial pipe tomahawk precious to its owner, a Seneca chief named Strong Bow. The Iroquois bitterly fought other tribes for the privilege of trading with Europeans for goods such as metal axes, knives, and hoes.

Door. In the summer of 1687, the Seneca were besieged by an army of 2,000 Frenchmen and Indians, including 140 Caughnawaga Mohawks, pressed into service on pain of imprisonment. As in the earlier French assault on the Mohawk, the large invasion force was easily detected by Iroquois scouts as it advanced; the chief of one scouting party, a Cayuga named Ourehouare, was captured by the attackers and dispatched along with 30 other prisoners to slave on French galleys in the Mediterranean. Unable to achieve surprise, the invaders had to content themselves with sacking empty Seneca villages. The Christian Mohawks of Caughnawaga, who had at first threatened desertion, were soon caught up in the fervor. After looting and burning four Seneca towns, the troops laid waste the ripening crops and full storehouses, destroying a year's worth of provisions. Some of the attackers desecrated Seneca burial grounds, defacing death masks and robbing graves. As a final insult, the troops removed the English coat of arms, which had been posted outside Iroquois towns to proclaim the empty promise of British protection.

The pillaging of the Seneca was just the first in a series of campaigns aimed at the Five Nations, whose angry counterstrokes only stiffened French resolve. In January 1693, an army of 600 French and Indian troops descended on the Mohawk with orders "to commit as great ravages as possible" around Albany. The British heard of the attack and hastily strengthened their own defenses without telling the Mohawk of the threat. "You tell us we are one heart, one flesh, and one blood," complained an Iroquois spokesman later. "Pray let us know the reason why you do not come to our assistance according to your former promise that we may live and die together?" The attack on Mohawk country was followed by a shaky truce, but in the summer of 1696, the French marched again, this time against the Oneida and Onondaga, taking care, as always, to destroy crops. "The enemy has brought us to a very low condition," said one Iroquois after surveying the damage done to the Keepers of the Central Fire. Worse was to come: In the late 1690s, the French prevailed on western Algonquians to attack the Five Nations repeatedly, reducing by hundreds the already-depleted ranks of Iroquois warriors.

With their military fortunes at a low ebb, the Iroquois turned with vigor to diplomacy. Amid all their troubles, the Five Nations were rallying politically. For the first time, they were functioning as a true confederacy, with leaders who met often to debate matters of import. Like the earlier league sachems, they continued to play a vital ceremonial role and promote internal harmony, but now they also addressed foreign policy. They did not always agree; some were inclined to break with the English and come to terms with the French, while others continued to look to Albany and the covenant chain for support. But as the 18th century dawned, a consensus emerged that it was time to end the disastrous cycle of conflict and reconcile the Five Nations to both European factions.

Weariness with war was evident throughout Iroquoia. In recent years, influential Clan Mothers had gone so far as to volunteer prized goods as peace offerings. At the same time, Iroquois who had kin among the Caughnawaga were reaching out to them in the hope of curbing the fratricidal strife; the Caughnawaga responded in kind and served as intermediaries in the ensuing talks between the Five Nations and the French. In 1700 and again in 1701, Iroquois delegations traveled to Montreal to talk peace while other councilors met with the English in Albany. Few Iroquois trusted the English as they once had: New York's new governor, the earl of Bellomont, found the chiefs he met with "so sullen and cold in their carriage that I thought we had quite lost their affections." Yet the English had to be humored if the confederacy hoped to maintain a position of neutrality between the two colonial rivals, whose troops had recently clashed in Nova Scotia and elsewhere along the coast and who remained deeply suspicious of each other's intentions.

A leading proponent of a neutralist policy for the Iroquois was the Onondaga chief Teganissorens. At Montreal, he pledged to suspend Iroquois raids if the French would grant the Iroquois ready access to their markets and to western hunting grounds. Despite the grumbling of western tribes, the French assented. Simultaneously, a delegation gathered in Albany, where the fastidious earl of Bellomont, who had earlier complained that the Iroquois seemed remote, found himself "shut up in a close chamber with 50 Sachems, who besides the stink of bear's grease with which they plentifully dawb'd themselves, were continually either smoking tobacco or drinking drams of rum."

The smoking and drinking did not distract the chiefs from their purpose. They asked the English to offer more for furs so as to attract pelts from western tribes and allow the Iroquois to serve as intermediaries. In return for English generosity—and protection in the event that peace with the French broke down—the Iroquois agreed in 1701 to deed to England's king all "that land where the beaver hunting is, which we won with the sword." In fact, the beleaguered Iroquois now had scant control over the vast western hunting ground that extended to Lake Michigan. But the for-

Captured by the French and their Indian allies in the summer of 1696, an Iroquois warrior stoically accepts his fate as his enemies prepare to burn him alive (background, before a tree). Watching the proceedings is a bearded Count Louis de Buade de Frontenac (right), governor general of Canada.

mal deed was useful to the English for future claims, and thus the Iroquois obliged their covenant-chain partners at little cost. Meanwhile, delegates to both Albany and Montreal were urging the Europeans to make peace with each other as well as with the confederacy. "Come, then, to some arrangement, both of you," implored the Iroquois at Montreal.

The payoff for these intricate maneuvers came in August 1701, when some 800 Indian delegates—including chiefs of the western tribes at odds with the Iroquois—met at Montreal to sign an accord. The deal nearly collapsed. First, western chiefs balked when they learned that the Iroquois had not brought captives to exchange as expected. Then illness swept the

assembly. But tradition won out. An old Wyandot chief, who had earlier sabotaged a French-Iroquois treaty, spoke from his deathbed,
urging his western allies to ratify the pact. After his death, two Iroquois delegates presided at his funeral. Harmony was restored, and
the leaders of 38 Indian peoples signed a treaty that gave the
former foes of the Iroquois the right to travel through the
Five Nations for trade. Separately, the Iroquois pledged
neutrality in any future wars between France and England. And the French agreed to let Iroquois hunt in
the west and barter at two key frontier posts. With
their backs to the wall, the Iroquois had made a
favorable settlement by deftly manipulating colonial authorities, who liked to think of themselves as masters of the diplomatic game.

The agreements gave the embattled Iroquois a chance to regroup. Although the English
and French continued at odds, the Iroquois—
with a few exceptions—remained neutral, hunting in the west and trading with their former enemies there. At the same time, European
missionaries, officials, and artisans were visiting
Iroquois villages. Blacksmiths were perhaps the
most welcome guests; the Iroquois were always
in need of craftsmen to repair tools and firearms.

Guns were still coveted; a new generation of
warriors was coming of age and foes lingered to
the south—groups the Iroquois, who wore their hair
high, called Flatheads. By 1707 Iroquois war parties were
ranging into the Carolinas to battle the Catawba and Cherokee. The feud grew so heated that a Seneca orator raged:
"The hatred I bear the Flatheads can never be forgiven."

Those sentiments were shared by another southern
tribe—the Tuscarora, Iroquoian speakers of North Carolina
who were being overpowered by white settlers in league with
the Catawba and Cherokee. At the behest of the Iroquois, some
2,000 Tuscaroras moved north in 1714 to live among the
Oneida. Eight years later, they were recognized as the sixth
Iroquois nation. Meanwhile, chiefs of the confederacy
were using their English ties to subordinate other groups.

*Mohawk statesman
Theyanoguin,
dubbed King Hen-
drick by the British,
wears European at-
tire given to him by
Queen Anne of Eng-
land during his trip
abroad in 1710.
Later, during the
French and Indian
War, he rallied Mo-
hawk support for
the British.*

By offering to protect Pennsylvania colonists from Indian raids, for example, they gained control over the Shawnee, Conoy, and Delaware. This coup, adroitly arranged by Teganissorens, expanded Iroquois hunting grounds and gave warriors a clear path to the hostile tribes farther south.

Even as Iroquois leaders were heartened by such gains, they looked with dismay on the escalating rivalry of the colonial powers, whose maneuvers seemed to be hedging in the Five Nations. In the 1720s, the French beefed up their post at Niagara; the English countered with a stronghold at the junction of the Oswego River and Lake Ontario. As one Iroquois chief protested to the English in the 1730s: "It is as if you on one side and the French on the other will press us out of our lands. We are like dumb people not knowing what ails us."

Other changes contributed to this feeling of uneasiness. In the darkness of a winter's night, elders still held youngsters spellbound with tales of Our Mother and the Good and Evil Twins. Families adhered to the principles of clan membership and matrilineal descent, as they had for centuries. And conclaves of the Great League were still marked by exchanges of wampum and words of condolence as in former times. But villagers had lost their foundations. The wars of the previous century had destroyed the main settlements, dispersing many Iroquois across a vast area from the Saint Lawrence in the north to the Susquehanna in the south and from the Hudson in the east to the Ohio Valley in the west. "All the six nations who are your brethren are scattered," a Mohawk spokesman told English officials in 1741. "A great number are gone to Canada and elsewhere, and those that are left we imagine will soon be gone."

Within these far-flung communities, few Iroquois still lived in longhouses; most occupied European-style cabins sheltering one or two families. Iroquois men hunted and fished rarely now; most bought goods at trading posts with money earned at odd jobs, portaging traders' canoes or carrying their packs. Alcohol, available at many trading posts, was taking a toll. Although some who drank sought spiritual intoxication, most did so to drown their frustrations—and the Iroquois had good reason to feel thwarted. Not only were their traditions eroding, so too was their territory, as it was bought, or stolen, by white farmers, lumbermen, and speculators. The Mohawk, closest to the colonial settlements, bore the brunt. "Our hearts grieve us when we consider what small parcel of land is remaining to us," Mohawk chiefs complained.

Soon the Iroquois would lose even the political unity they had fostered with such care. In 1754 the long-smoldering conflict between the English and French erupted anew. In this bitter nine-year struggle—known to the English, who triumphed, as the French and Indian War—the Iroquois again were tragically divided. To the east, the Mohawk sided with the English, while to the west, the Seneca lined up with the French and their native allies, whose ranks included many so-called mission Iroquois—descendants of the original Caughnawaga, along with more recent exiles to French territory who had embraced Catholicism. Elsewhere, the Iroquois tried to preserve neutrality, but few were left untouched.

Among those reluctantly embroiled in the struggle was an elderly Mohawk statesman known as Chief Theyanoguin, or King Hendrick to the English. A Protestant convert and staunch supporter of the covenant chain, he had visited England as a young man as part of an Indian delegation to the royal court. After his return, Hendrick helped promote Protestantism among the Mohawk and kept faith with his English allies at councils. As colonists encroached on Mohawk territory, however, Theyanoguin came to feel betrayed. In 1753, at a meeting between Mohawk leaders and New York's governor, he angrily cataloged incidents in which land had been stolen from the Iroquois and declared, "The covenant chain is broken between you and us." His English brothers should not expect to hear from the Mohawk anymore, he added, "and we desire to hear no more of you." Despite his words, Theyanoguin threw his support to the English when war broke out, perhaps hoping that loyalty to the covenant chain would allow the Iroquois to retain authority over other Indians. "We are the six confederate Indian nations," he proclaimed proudly to companions during the war, "the heads and superiors of all Indian nations of the continent of America."

As he spoke, Theyanoguin was preparing to lead the Mohawk into battle against the French and their Indian allies. Camped near Lake George in September 1755 with English troops commanded by General William Johnson, Hendrick was asked by Johnson to commit 200 Mohawk warriors to a reconnaissance against an army thought to number several thousand, among them many mission Iroquois. The old chief obliged, although he was skeptical of the plan. "If they are to be killed, they are too many," he said of his men. "If they are to fight, they are too few."

His fears were borne out. A little later, his column was ambushed, and he lost his life. The side he fought and died for was victorious, but the spoils for the Iroquois would be measured in misfortune. ◆

Early Indian players, sticks aloft, vie for the ball in a vivid sculpture by Jud Hartmann that stands outside the Lacrosse Hall of Fame in Baltimore. An inscription at the statue's base announces that it was erected to "forever honor the Iroquois" from whom "the modern game of lacrosse most directly descends."

THE LEGACY OF LACROSSE

Lacrosse, a sport currently played around the world, originated with the Native Americans centuries before the first Europeans arrived in North America. According to Iroquois tradition, the game was an ancient gift from the Creator, a divine contest to be played for his pleasure and propitiation. Athletes took to the field to settle communal disputes, to beseech the spirits to send down rain for the spring corn, or to ask for divine help in healing the sick.

Early European explorers were astonished to witness hundreds of players competing on fields that stretched for more than a mile. It was a French missionary who in the 1600s gave the sport its present name, noting that the bent sticks used by the Indians resembled a bishop's crook, or crosier.

Popular among many disparate tribes, lacrosse was a special passion of the Iroquois, and it was their version that gave rise to the modern sport. By the mid-1800s, Iroquois teams were playing matches and spreading enthusiasm for the game in Montreal and other parts of Canada, in several cities in the United States, and then in Great Britain. By 1878 lacrosse had reached Australia and New Zealand.

Native American teams were barred in 1880 from international amateur competition because some of them had accepted expense money for their trips. It was not until the 1980s that the Iroquois reentered the global arena. Since that time, all-star Iroquois teams have taken part in the World Games and other international tournaments, proudly playing the sport that has remained, as a great Iroquois player has said, "ingrained in our culture and our lives."

Playing their own ancient form of lacrosse, scores of Choctaw men swarm across an Arkansas prairie in an 1830s painting by George Catlin. The artist marveled at the sight of hundreds of players "running together and leaping, actually over each other's heads, and darting between their adversaries' legs" as they tried to score by carrying the ball between the tall goalposts at opposite ends of the field.

The 19th-century stick above, used when the first games between Iroquois and white teams were played, is made of bent hickory with a pocket of woven rawhide. The 1840s wooden ball, the size of a grapefruit, is larger than today's hard rubber balls.

Members of the lacrosse club of Caughnawaga—part of the Iroquois treaty territory in Canada—gather for a photograph in 1867, the year the club defeated a Montreal team in a game honoring the adoption of lacrosse as the national sport of Canada.

Iroquois players wearing striped uniforms battle a Canadian team for the ball in an 1876 engraving depicting a match played in Ireland. Teams of Iroquois visited Ireland and Great Britain several times during the 1870s and 1880s, holding popular exhibition matches; several of the English and Scottish lacrosse clubs that were organized at the time are still in operation today.

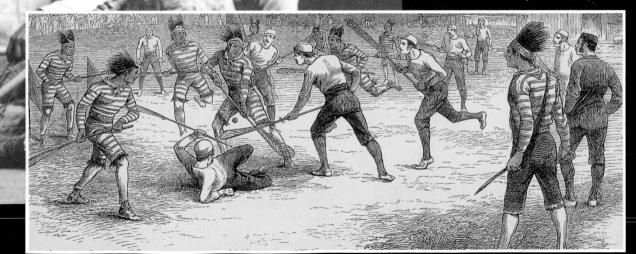

A wide-mouthed, short-handled goal-keeper's stick employed by Onondaga lacrosse star Oren Lyons, Jr., seen at right center, is now enshrined in the Lacrosse Hall of Fame.

Three expert Iroquois players of the modern era, Laverne Doctor, Jr. (left), Oren Lyons, and Howard Hill, wear the jersey of their Indian team, the Onondaga Athletic Club, in a photograph that was taken in 1953. Lyons went on to play for the undefeated 1957 team at Syracuse University, long a powerhouse of American lacrosse. He subsequently became a chief of the Iroquois confederacy's Grand Council, and was inducted into the Lacrosse Hall of Fame on February 6, 1993.

Two Indian teams, the Onondaga Athletic Club and the Syracuse Warriors, compete in box lacrosse, an abbreviated form of the sport that is usually played in the confines of ice rinks during the hockey off-season. Box lacrosse employs fewer players than traditional outdoor field lacrosse—six men a side instead of 10—and is marked by swift, pinpoint passing of the ball.

An Iroquois player scrambles for the ball in a 1990 game at Perth against Team USA. The Iroquois team's appearance in Australia marked its return to international competition after a ban of more than a century.

The Iroquois flag flies alongside those of Australia and the International Lacrosse Federation during the 1990 world championships held in Perth. The Iroquois banner is modeled after the ancient Hiawatha wampum belt, which symbolizes the union of nations within the Iroquois confederacy.

HY

A stylized image of an Iroquois eagle dancer, symbol of strength and power, forms the logo of the Iroquois Nationals, an all-Indian team that has played in many international tournaments.

Thayeadanegea,
Joseph Brant
the Mohawk Chief.

THE SHATTERED CONFEDERACY

Joseph Brant, the Mohawk chief who fought for the British against the American colonists, appears here at the age of 33 in a portrait painted in 1776 by George Romney. As a youth, Brant was a frequent guest of the British trader and colonial official Sir William Johnson, who made his home in Mohawk territory. Their alliance was sealed when Brant's sister Molly became Johnson's common-law wife.

In the summer of 1768, Sir William Johnson sent out belts of wampum inviting representatives of the Six Nations and other tribes to a council at Fort Stanwix, a redoubt built by the British a decade earlier on the site of present-day Rome, New York. The fort overlooked a 15-mile-wide strip of land the Iroquois called De-o-waint-sta, or "Great Carrying Place," which served as the portage between the Mohawk River and Oneida Lake, a gateway to the west. The purpose of the meeting was to negotiate a new border between Indian territory and the area open to white settlement. A line had been established by royal proclamation along the crest of the Appalachians five years before. But now Sir William, as British superintendent of Indian affairs for the northern department, wanted to extend the boundary much farther west.

Sir William had mixed emotions about the proposal. He was a long-time intimate of the Iroquois, especially the Mohawk, among whom he had lived for 30 years, raising a family of six children with his Mohawk common-law wife, Molly Brant. As a general during the French and Indian War, he had been ably assisted by Iroquois, including the late Chief Theyanoguin, and he wanted to protect the Indians from the worst excesses of the colonists. But he was also a prominent landowner who stood to profit handsomely from a new agreement. During the weeks leading up to the meeting, he had presided over a bonanza of claims by colleagues and other private speculators amounting to hundreds of thousands of acres in the proposed region of cession. All of these purchases depended upon successful negotiation of the new boundary.

The Iroquois filing into Fort Stanwix shared a realistic view of their prospects. They realized that their confederacy no longer held the balance of power in the Northeast; with the British expulsion of France from the continent, they could no longer play off one European power against the other. There was no need of Iroquois middlemen between Albany and the western tribes, who could now trade directly with the British. And a recent Indian attempt to drive the British from the Great Lakes area, led by Pontiac, had failed—despite the fact that the great Ottawa leader had broad support among other Indians in the area, including the Seneca, the confederacy's Keeper of the Western Door and its largest community.

Rivalry among whites now took the form of animosity between King George III and the colonists, who no longer needed British protection against France and its Indian allies. Many Virginians already had settled west of the Appalachians in violation of the royal proclamation. The Iroquois saw this encroachment as a *fait accompli* and were ready to accept it in return for proper payment. But they also hoped that the concessions Sir William wanted would be the last. "Let us make a line for the benefit of our children," one sachem urged, "that they may have lands which cannot be taken from them and let us doing that show the king that we are generous, and that we will leave him land enough for his people, then he will regard us, and take better care that his people do not cheat us."

Delegates to the council began arriving in the early fall. There were representatives from the colonies of Virginia, Pennsylvania, New Jersey, and New York. Indian delegates included not only members of the Six Nations, but also the Catholic Caughnawaga from the Jesuit mission at Laprairie, Quebec, the Conoy and Nanticoke from the Susquehanna River region, and the Mingo, Shawnee, and Delaware from the Ohio country. Sir William was prepared. Boats came up the Mohawk bearing 60 barrels of flour, 50 barrels of pork, 6 barrels of rice, 70 barrels of other provisions, and many casks of rum to be locked in the fort's strongroom. His experience suggested that at such meetings an Indian consumed twice as much as a white man. "It cannot be supposed," he wrote later, "that hungry Indians can be kept here, or in any temper, without a bellyful."

More than 3,000 Indians—perhaps the greatest such assemblage in the continent's history—were present when Sir William opened the meeting on October 24. Despite the marked changes in the basis of the relationship between the British and the Six Nations, he invoked the old image of the covenant chain, claiming he intended to strengthen it by "rubbing off any rust which it may have contracted that it may appear bright to all nations as a proof of our love and friendship."

The negotiations proceeded for 13 days. Finally, on November 5, the Iroquois agreed to a boundary that cut west from the Susquehanna and ran down along the Allegheny and Ohio rivers to the Tennessee River, just 30 miles short of the Mississippi. Everything west of the boundary was recognized as Indian territory. The Iroquois conceded the vast lands to the south and east of the line—large parts of present-day Tennessee,

Pressed by white settlers and speculators, the Six Nations were eventually deprived of much of their ancestral territory, including sacred spots such as Cohoes Falls near Albany, celebrated in Iroquois lore as the site where Hiawatha and Deganawida met and conceived the Great League of Peace.

Kentucky, West Virginia, Pennsylvania, and New York—even though that territory included the historic hunting grounds of other native groups, notably the Shawnee and Delaware, who resented the fact that the Iroquois had used their influence with the English to claim jurisdiction over them.

A chief from each of the Six Nations made his mark on the treaty to signify acceptance. A steel used to strike sparks stood for the Mohawk, a tree for the Oneida, a cross for the Tuscarora, a hill for the Onondaga, a pipe for the Cayuga, and a high hill for the Seneca. The purchase price was displayed in the square of the fort and consisted of blankets, kettles, knives, brooches, and silver coins worth about $50,000.

The Treaty of Fort Stanwix was the first in a series of agreements to be negotiated over the next three decades that the Iroquois regarded as formal white recognition of their right to exist as sovereign nations. "We hope that what we have said will not be forgotten," an Iroquois speaker said six years later, "for we remember it still, and you have it all in writing." But the treaty ignored two explosive issues. One was the anger of the Shawnee and other Ohio Indians, whom the Iroquois had betrayed by selling off their hunting grounds, a betrayal that would undermine Iroquois influence. The other issue was fraught with greater peril: the growing resistance of the colonists to proclamations that infringed on their

freedom to seek land to the west, regardless of Indian claims. Despite recent opposition to the British among the Seneca, the fortunes of the Iroquois depended more than ever on their covenant chain with the Crown—one whose links were corroding and would soon be broken.

The frailty of the new treaty quickly became apparent. Colonists in the back country flouted its terms by setting up homesteads on Indian land. The Crown's governor of Virginia, Lord Dunmore, vigorously encouraged the illegal settlements, often at a handsome profit from land speculation. The governor's policies helped lead in the spring of 1774 to that "brief orgy of irresponsibility, cruelty, and despair," as one historian of the Iroquois later described it, the conflict known as Lord Dunmore's War.

British officials and Iroquois representatives gather outside Johnson Hall, built in 1755 by Sir William Johnson near the Mohawk River. After Sir William's death in 1774, his nephew Guy Johnson (inset)—shown wearing moccasins and other native handiwork—assumed his uncle's post as superintendent of Indian affairs for the northern colonies. Artist Benjamin West included a shadowy Indian in the background to emphasize the Johnson family's ties to the Iroquois.

The fighting was triggered by a Virginia militia captain, Michael Cresap, and a group of land speculators. While exploring south of the Ohio River in an area that had been bought from the Iroquois at Fort Stanwix, Cresap's group lost some horses. They immediately blamed the Shawnee, who had refused to accept the provisions of Fort Stanwix, and were still hunting in the area. Cresap came upon a peaceful party of three Shawnees and massacred them.

A few days later, some of his fellow Virginians committed another atrocity. When Indians from a village near present-day Steubenville, Ohio, crossed the river to buy milk from a settler, a gang of frontiersmen gave them whiskey, got them drunk, and then killed most of them. Among the dead were the father, brother, and sister of a Cayuga chief named John Logan. Logan had immigrated to the Ohio country, married a Shawnee, and built a reputation as a friend of white settlers. Soon two other prominent Indians were murdered by whites, Bald Eagle, a Seneca who lived with the Delaware, and Silver Heels, a Shawnee chief.

Vowing revenge, a group of Delawares, Shawnees, and Mingoes descended on white settlements along the Virginia frontier. Logan led the way, obligated by custom to avenge his family members. He and a party of eight warriors fell upon a small settlement of white families who had usurped Indian lands on the Muskingum River in present-day Ohio and killed a number of men, women, and children.

As the smoldering frontier burst into flame during that summer of 1774, Logan asked his fellow Iroquois for support. Some Senecas, outraged by the killing of Bald Eagle, joined the Ohio bands. Protesting the actions of the Virginians to Sir William Johnson, the sachems of the Six

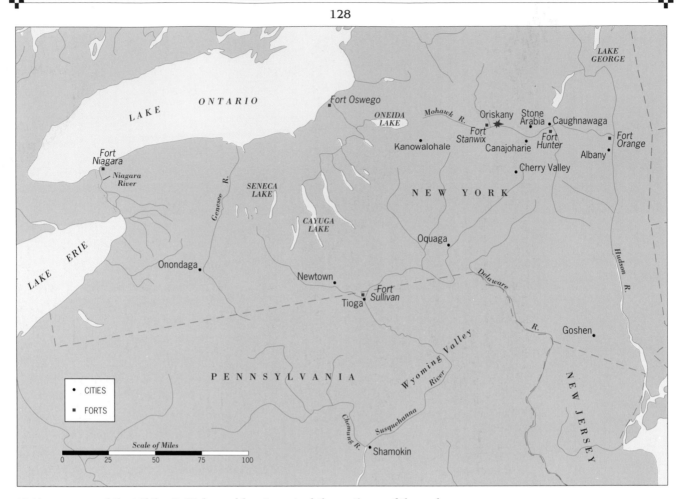

Nations warned that if the British could not control the actions of the colonists, "we must look upon every agreement you made with us as void."

In July the Iroquois sachems and 600 followers met with Johnson at his estate on the Mohawk River. Some of them were angry enough to heed Logan's call for warriors. Sir William, already under stress from feeble health at age 59, made a strenuous effort to dissuade them from hostile action. He was especially concerned about the Seneca, who had traditionally exerted much influence over the nations of the Ohio country. Scorning an interpreter, Sir William was addressing the sachems in the arbor behind his house when he was stricken with a massive heart attack. To the dismay of the assemblage, he died shortly thereafter.

Sir William's carefully groomed successor, his nephew Guy Johnson, who had come over from Ireland as a young man, presided at a subsequent council in September. Johnson had the confidence of the sachems, who named him Uraghquadirha, or "Rays of the Sun Enlightening the Earth." Bringing with them the wampum belt that signified the covenant chain, they assured Johnson that the chain had been kept "clean from rust." With these symbolic words, the Iroquois pledged peace and reaffirmed their longstanding alliance with the British.

The Grand Council of the confederacy—as that peacekeeping and policymaking assembly of 50 titleholders was now known—met at Onon-

The American Revolution devastated the Iroquois confederacy, pitting those who sided with the rebellious colonists against those who remained loyal to the British and subjecting both sides to fierce reprisals. This map shows the sites of major battles involving the Iroquois as well as important Iroquois settlements in 1776, most of which were destroyed during the conflict.

daga in October to ratify the decision to stay out of the fray. The sachems censured the Cayuga for allowing a small war party to join the fighting and agreed to try to persuade the Shawnee to bury the hatchet, as they put it. By the time the council adjourned, these actions proved academic. Lord Dunmore had raised more than 1,500 militiamen and, while the sachems solemnly conferred, concluded his brief war by routing the outnumbered Shawnee and their allies at Point Pleasant in western Virginia.

Although the deliberations of the Grand Council had been ineffectual, the confederacy had managed nonetheless to demonstrate a staunch unity, an achievement that was largely due to a recent concession by the war chiefs of the Six Nations to be bound by the decisions of the sachems. Such firm resolve had not been seen for many years, and it would now be tested by the burgeoning crisis between the Crown and its colonists. Disaffected Americans, protesting new taxes and trade regulations, had already formed a government, known as the Continental Congress; soon members of the Six Nations would be perplexed by the sight of the English speakers killing one another instead of Indians or Frenchmen.

Both sides wooed the Indians. The Iroquois were considered pivotal because of their military prowess and strategic location. Loyalists and rebels were content at first to let the Six Nations remain neutral, but as war approached, the race to recruit allies quickened. In competing for Iroquois allegiance, the British had numerous advantages. They could point to the old covenant chain and to their attempts to uphold Indian land claims. In addition, unlike the impecunious Americans, the royal treasury could afford the guns, axes, kettles, spinning cloth, blankets, and other trade goods upon which the Iroquois had grown dependent. Old ties with the Johnson family also played a role. Molly Brant, widow of the late Sir William, exerted great influence as a matriarch of the Turtle Clan and proved to be one of King George III's most effective agents among the Mohawk. "One word from her," said Daniel Claus, Sir William's former deputy, "goes further with them than a thousand from any white man."

The Americans countered by arguing that they were the legitimate heirs to the old covenant-chain connection. They held numerous councils with representatives of the Six Nations, prepared wampum belts, and made copious promises of gifts that they could not always deliver.

Despite their ties to the British, most Iroquois wanted to remain neutral. "We love you both—old England and new," a group of Oneidas told the governor of Connecticut early in 1775. More than sentiment motivated the sachems. For a while at least, many hoped to resume the old mid-

dleman role that had served them
so well with the French and British.
But after armed conflict broke out
in April 1775 in Massachusetts and
Virginia, neutrality began to give
way. Not all the pressures were external. Two men with strong fol-
lowings among the Iroquois—one
white and a man of God, the other
Indian and a warrior—added to the
growing factionalism.

The apostle of the American
rebels was the Reverend Samuel
Kirkland. A solemn New England
Congregationalist with a self-
described "peculiar affection for
Indians," Kirkland had been working among the Oneida and Tuscarora since 1766. He and his Indian
assistants taught school, demonstrated agricultural techniques, settled quarrels, and provided food to
needy families. His worship services so impressed the Indians that
several hundred congregants typically showed up from a half-dozen

Two 18th-century French watercolors depict
a Mohawk woman in traditional dress and a
Mohawk warrior. The woman is shown with
a finger-woven strap, or tumpline, around
her forehead, used to support the basket on
her back. The man carries a tomahawk and
wears the body paint and single scalp lock
that mark him as a fighter.

or so villages around Oneida Lake. When the meeting place overflowed,
some of them willingly stood outside in the snow for the entire three-
hour service. Kirkland won their affection despite his strict doctrines and
insistence upon sobriety. By challenging the old religious beliefs of the
Tuscarora and Oneida, he weakened the traditional political structure
headed by the sachems, who had recently been trying to rein in the war
chiefs. At the same time, the militant Kirkland won support among the
warriors. "Numbers of them," he wrote, "said they would go with me to
prison or death—where I followed Christ, they would follow."

His sway over the warriors and his pro-American independence activities worried the British. In 1775 Kirkland testified before the Continental Congress in Philadelphia. He then returned home to interpret the proceedings for his parishioners. Guy Johnson was so incensed that he

threatened to cut off aid to any native group that harbored Kirkland. Nevertheless, the missionary's campaigning proved so effective that by early June 1776, he could report to Major General Philip Schuyler, the newly appointed American Indian commissioner, that the Oneida and Tuscarora had resolved "that if the others join the king's party, they would die with the Americans in the contest."

The Mohawk who took the lead in tugging the Iroquois from the opposite direction was Molly Brant's younger brother Thayendanegea, known to whites as Joseph Brant. A protégé of Sir William's, Brant had been a classmate of Kirkland's in the early 1760s at a Connecticut school that instructed prospective white missionaries and a few promising young Indians. The two young men got along well together—Brant tutored Kirkland in the Mohawk tongue while refining his own command of English, which he added to his mastery of other languages of the Six Nations. As a faithful Anglican, Brant later worked to translate the New Testament into Mohawk.

By 1775 Brant and Kirkland were at odds, with Brant joining other prominent Mohawks in supporting Guy Johnson and his king. In the spring of that year, the former schoolmates crossed paths at Fort Stanwix, where Kirkland was set upon by Indians hostile to the American cause. Although Brant shared their sentiments, he intervened to protect Kirkland. As the missionary wrote later, Brant told the assailants that while they might well consider Kirkland "ungrateful to our king, he thinks he does his duty toward his country. Let him then be considered as our enemy, but do not kill him."

A few months later, Brant and a group of Mohawks—pressured by rebel settlers who were seizing their lands in the Mohawk Valley—accompanied Guy Johnson to the safer confines of Canada. There, in September, in a battle at Saint Johns, just north of Lake Champlain, Brant and his fellow Mohawks helped the British delay the short-lived American invasion of Canada.

Eager to investigate the depth of the British commitment to the Iroquois, Brant sailed for England with Johnson in November 1775. Like his grandfather, who had gone there in 1710 during Queen Anne's time, Brant took London by storm. Now 33 years old, he cut a handsome figure with his urbane manner, good looks, and raven hair gathered in a queue like that of fashionable white men. His grievances about land that had been taken from the Mohawk got a sympathetic hearing from the colonial secretary. Brant was presented to King George III, initiated into the Masons, and lionized by high society. The artist George Romney painted his portrait, and a journalist named James Boswell, future biographer of Samuel Johnson, interviewed him, later expressing disappointment that the well-educated Mohawk lacked "the ferocious dignity of a savage leader."

Brant sailed for New York in June 1776, convinced more than ever that the interests of the Iroquois resided with the Crown. When American privateers attacked his ship, Brant and a Mohawk companion shot several American crewmen with the new brass rifles that had been presented to them in London. When they docked in New York, the American Revolution was in full swing, and Brant joined in the successful British campaign to drive General George Washington's army from the city. Then he

Brant received this metal gorget emblazoned with a royal crest from English officials during a visit to London. Worn at the neck, gorgets were not only a traditional part of British military regalia but also time-honored Indian adornments.

made his way back to Iroquois country, where he told his fellow Mohawks about his travels across the sea and urged them to join the British in their planned campaign through upstate New York. On the Susquehanna River at Oquaga, he raised a force of more than 100 fighting men. Scarcely a score of them were Mohawk warriors; most were white men loyal to the Crown. Serving without pay as Brant's Volunteers, these Tories donned war paint and dressed Indian style.

Faced with the conflicting demands of men such as Brant and Kirkland, the sachems of the Grand Council had little chance of maintaining a united front in the best of circumstances. As it happened, an epidemic of unknown origin conspired to undermine their peacekeeping efforts. In January 1777, disease struck the Iroquois seat at Onondaga, claiming three sachems among its 90 victims and forcing the extinguishing of the council fire that had long burned there. The Grand Council adjourned, and before new leaders could be installed, the Iroquois yielded to partisan pressures. In July warriors from the Seneca, Cayuga, Onondaga, and Mohawk nations convened at British request near Oswego, on the shores of Lake Ontario. After days of listening to British entreaties to the old covenant chain and receiving enticements of rum and material goods, the warriors voted to ally with King George III. In taking up the hatchet against the Americans, those four nations were also turning against their recalcitrant brothers, the Oneida and Tuscarora. The confederacy had foundered on the rock of the American Revolution.

Soon Iroquois were deeply embroiled in the conflict, sometimes on opposite sides of the lines. In the summer of 1777, the British launched a three-pronged offensive aimed at isolating New England. One column was to sail up the Hudson River from New York City; a second marched south from Canada toward Albany; a third, comprising about 1,700 men—more than half of them Indians—headed east from Oswego along the old river-and-lake trade route with the aim of capturing Fort Stanwix and linking up with the other columns at Albany.

The Indian contingent of the Fort Stanwix column included Senecas, Mohawks, Joseph Brant's Volunteers, and a number of Algonquian-speaking Mississaugas from Canada. According to some accounts, the Senecas harbored old doubts about the wisdom of supporting the British and agreed to go along simply as observers. As noted by Mary Jemison, a white captive who had been adopted by the Seneca, the British "stated

Pipe in hand, the Seneca chief Cornplanter exudes a serene determination in this portrait made after the American Revolution, during which he sided with the British. Speaking before the United States Congress in Philadelphia in 1790, he made efforts at reconciliation, saying, "It is my wish and the wishes of my people to live peaceably and quietly with you and yours, but the losses we have sustained require some compensation."

that they did not wish to have them fight, but wanted to have them just sit down, smoke their pipes, and look on."

But the Senecas and other Indians, Jemison added, were soon "obliged to fight for their lives." On August 5, their column—rounded out by British regulars, loyal colonists, and Hessian mercenaries—had surrounded Fort Stanwix and its 700-man garrison when a Mohawk messenger arrived. He had alarming news from Joseph Brant's sister, Molly, who was still living at her home in Canajoharie in the Mohawk Valley and keeping her eye on the rebels there. She reported that some 800 American militiamen under General Nicholas Herkimer were en route to relieve Fort Stanwix. To intercept them, the British commander, Lieutenant Colonel Barry St. Leger, dispatched Sir John Johnson, son of the late Sir William, with a force of about 70 whites and 400 Indians, including Joseph Brant. Johnson selected an ambush site in a marshy ravine near Oriskany Creek, five miles from the fort, and set the stage for one of the bloodiest single engagements of the American Revolution.

The next morning, the Americans marched headlong toward the trap. Although General Herkimer was accompanied by 60 Oneida men and women who knew the territory intimately, he failed to take the slightest precautions. When his column blindly followed the trail into the ravine, the Indians hiding in the woods on the flanks opened fire with their muskets. Then they charged, shouting war whoops, swinging war clubs and tomahawks, and thrusting with spears. Brant and his Mohawks pursued those who fled and cut them down. The Oneida warrior Blatcop retaliated by charging across the field three times, slashing left and right with his tomahawk. Honyery Doxtater, an Oneida war chief, suffered a wound in the right wrist but kept firing his musket while his wife loaded the weapon—and fired off a few rounds with her own.

Many of Herkimer's force escaped the ravine and took up positions behind trees on a plateau to the west. As soon as one of the Mohawks heard a musket discharge, he would rush in to cut down whoever had fired it. To thwart this, the Americans put two men behind a tree. When the unsuspecting Indian jumped forward to dispatch a militiaman in the act of reloading, the second American would fire at him point-blank. But the Indians kept coming, demonstrating, as one of the British commanders reported, "the greatest zeal for His Majesty's cause." Senecas found themselves in the thick of the fighting, and gave their all. The Seneca warrior Blacksnake later likened the bloodshed to "a stream running down on the descending ground."

The Indians fighting on the side of the British won the day by preventing the Americans from relieving the fort. And while they paid a price—62 killed or wounded—they exacted a higher one from the enemy, who suffered an appalling 500 casualties, including General Herkimer, who died after the amputation of a wounded leg. A number of Americans were taken prisoner and forced to run the gantlet by the Indians, who clubbed many of them to death. The British laid siege to Fort Stanwix, but lacked sufficient artillery to conquer the stronghold and abandoned the effort 16 days later.

The Battle of Oriskany proved significant to the Iroquois. That success hardened the determination of the Seneca to carry on the war and widened the rift within the confederacy. After the battle, pro-British Iroquois burned an Oneida settlement near Oriskany; Oneidas and rebels pillaged the Mohawk village of Canajoharie, including the home of Molly Brant, who escaped. In September, the Oneida and Tuscarora declared war on the British and their allies in the confederacy. Like the whites, the Iroquois would remain divided throughout the war.

While relatively few Oneidas and Tuscaroras joined Washington's army, the pro-British Iroquois played a more significant role, mainly as raiders. The warriors took the winter off to hunt and provide for their families. Then, in the spring, fighting bands of both Indians and Loyalists formed, ranging in size from a dozen men to as many as 500. Starting in the spring of 1778, they roamed the countryside from northern Pennsylvania to the Mohawk Valley, terrorizing frontier settlements. Told by the British to drive away American farmers and deprive the colonies of food, the raiders burned houses, destroyed grain mills, and torched the fields.

Several chiefs rose to prominence during these raids. Two of the most effective were Senecas—Cornplanter, who probably was in his early forties, and a weathered warrior in his seventies known as Old Smoke. Cornplanter, of mixed parentage, was so admired by his warriors that when they unknowingly burned down the house of his Dutch father and then took the old man captive, they convened a council and agreed—"as a compliment to Cornplanter," said the warrior Blacksnake—to free the father and most other prisoners taken on the raid. Old Smoke, who received his name from the mist of Indian summer that vanishes during the

Two silver brooches produced by Iroquois metalworkers exemplify the European-inspired objects artisans of the Six Nations turned out for Iroquois use as the fur trade declined and such items were no longer being obtained from whites for pelts. The brooch opposite incorporates the compass-and-arc design of the Masonic emblem, popularized by Joseph Brant, who joined the Masons.

heat of the day, often had to ride a horse because of his age but served with distinction throughout the war.

During the summer of 1778, Cornplanter and Old Smoke jointly led a foray in the Wyoming Valley of Pennsylvania that resulted in perhaps the most one-sided action of the war. Their 464 Seneca and Cayuga warriors, augmented by 110 Tories, destroyed eight forts, burned nearly 1,000 homes, drove away 1,000 head of livestock, and massacred more than 300 militiamen. Indian losses amounted to fewer than a dozen men.

The Mohawk Joseph Brant remained the most talked-about Indian raider of the Revolution, however. He was idolized by his British superiors for his dependability and savvy and demonized by the Americans, who referred to him as "monster Brant." Such was Brant's notoriety that survivors of the Wyoming massacre blamed him for the atrocities—"the most horrid scenes of savage barbarity," according to one report—although Brant was not even present during the raid.

In fact, Brant generally conducted himself with the same sense of honor he had shown earlier in sparing Reverend Kirkland. At Goshen, New York, in July 1779, he intervened to save the life of an American captain named John Wood—who had inadvertently shown the Masonic sign of distress by clasping his hands above his head—and then continued to protect him even after Wood admitted that he was not a member of the fraternal order. In a raid on the settlement at Cherry Valley, where 32 noncombatants were slain by his fellow Mohawks, the quick-witted Brant rescued a Loyalist woman and her five children from rampaging Senecas by marking each of them with his red war paint, a sign that they were his captives and should not be tampered with.

But Brant and his fellow Iroquois raiders remained infamous in the eyes of the Americans. Determined to give the Indians a dose of their own medicine, General George Washington mounted a campaign to ravage Iroquois country in 1779. His orders were blunt: "to lay waste all the settlements around that the country may not be merely overrun but destroyed."

A preliminary American strike that spring destroyed three Onondaga settlements. The raid wiped out the place where the council fire had burned, alienating many Onondagas who had been rent by

British dignitaries honored their Iroquois ally Joseph Brant with an assortment of gifts, including this tomahawk with a silver plaque bearing the inscription, "Given to my friend Joseph Brant from the Duke of Northumberland 1805."

conflicting sentiments—pro-British, pro-American, and neutralist. Then, in late summer, one American column moved up the Allegheny River, and two larger ones joined forces at Tioga, a Seneca village on the Chemung River. This expedition, led by Major General John Sullivan, marched up the river with more than 4,000 men and an artillery train of perhaps 13 guns. The cannon paid off a few days later at Newtown, when some 600 Tories and Indians, including Brant and Cornplanter, attempted a stand and were forced to flee under a barrage of shot and iron spikes.

Sullivan's army advanced like a wave of locusts, destroying everything in its 270-mile-long path to the Genesee River and back. The cannon, noted Sergeant John Salmon of New Jersey, were fired morning and evening to notify the Indian villages ahead of the army's progress, allowing the inhabitants to flee before its arrival. The soldiers expressed amazement at the sturdy cabins and substantial farms of these people they considered uncivilized—and proceeded to ruin all they could. They burned more than 40 Seneca and Cayuga hamlets. They chopped down apple and peach orchards, laid waste stores of beans, squash, and other vegetables, and scorched cornfields, destroying thousands of bushels of corn. By collecting scalps, and displaying at least one pair of leggings fashioned from the skin of dead Indians, the expedition amassed its own share of the kind of barbarities the whites usually attributed to the Iroquois. Washington's orders had been carried out so efficiently that the Iroquois thereafter called him the "town destroyer."

More than 5,000 Iroquois and other Indians took refuge at Fort Niagara—and fought back ferociously. Huddling in tents and huts, dependent upon the British for food, they survived one of the worst winters in memory and returned to the warpath in the spring of 1780. For three more years, bands from a force of nearly 900 warriors, led by Brant, Cornplanter, and others, joined Loyalist forces to ravage a broad swath of settlements from the Mohawk River west to the Ohio. In the process, they destroyed the shelters of their Oneida and Tuscarora brethren, including Samuel Kirkland's old church in Kanowalohale.

Iroquois war parties continued raiding right up to the summer of 1783 and the discovery that in faraway Paris the British had signed a peace treaty. The treaty turned over to the Americans everything south of Canada and east of the Mississippi, including the lands reserved for Indian

occupation under the Fort Stanwix agreement of 1768. It said not a single word about Indians. In an impassioned speech to General Frederick Haldimand, the British governor in Quebec, Joseph Brant reminded his ally that the Iroquois had been first among the Indians to recognize the English as friends and brothers. "We were then a great People," he remarked, "and you in a manner but a handful." He closed by asking whether the British would vouch for Iroquois claims to "those lands which the great being above has pointed out for our ancestors and their descendants, and where the bones of our forefathers are laid," or whether the blood of the remaining Iroquois would now be shed and mingled with those bones, through the neglect of "our allies for whom we have so often freely bled?" There was little that General Haldimand could say in response. The Crown that generations of Iroquois had backed with such courage and effectiveness had abandoned them.

If the American Revolution had brought distress to the Iroquois, the

A misleading engraving inspired by the abuse American colonists heaped on Brant shows him, tomahawk in hand, leading the massacre of soldiers and settlers in Pennsylvania's Wyoming Valley in 1778. Thomas Campbell, who attributed the deed in verse to "monster Brant," later conceded that Brant was far from the scene at the time.

aftermath threatened to plunge them into utter despair. The war had scattered the people and so ravaged their homeland that only two villages remained unscathed. And its legacy endured in a chain of lethal events—death by starvation, exposure, disease, and violence—that swept like a scythe through the Iroquois. In a period of 20 years, the the Six Nations' population was reduced from its prewar level of around 9,000 to roughly half that number.

A series of postwar treaties imposed by the victorious Americans completed the breakup of what had been a separate Iroquois state. These agreements stripped the Iroquois of their remaining diplomatic rights and military power and deprived them of much of their ancestral land. The direction was clearly established in 1784 during negotiations for a new Treaty of Fort Stanwix. Here, where the Iroquois had negotiated as equals with the British, representatives of the new republic asserted the political sovereignty of the United States over all native peoples within its new border. The terms of the treaty forced the Iroquois to cede all claims to the Ohio country and even to provide hostages until the last of the prisoners taken by the pro-British Iroquois had been returned.

As this drama was being played out, many Iroquois anticipated the outcome and cast their lot with the British in Canada, dividing the confederacy as never before. Through the winter and spring of 1785, Joseph Brant, after seeing his old homeland in the Mohawk Valley occupied by Americans, led an exodus of Iroquois into Canada, where four other small settlements of Mohawks already existed. The most recent had been established on the north shore of Lake Ontario by John Deserontyon, who had fled to Montreal with about 100 Mohawks early in the war.

The Brant group was far larger. After a few months, it numbered more than 1,800, including most of the surviving Mohawks and a number of Cayugas, along with others from the Six Nations and even a handful of Delawares, Creeks, and other Indians who had sided with the British dur-

The Seneca orator Red Jacket—so called for the scarlet coat he wore as an ally of the British during the Revolution—appears in a different guise in this 1829 painting by George Catlin. Around his neck is a medal that was presented to him by George Washington in 1792 when he called on the American president with other Iroquois chiefs.

The engraved silver peace medal given to Red Jacket in 1792 shows George Washington offering a pipe to an Iroquois as a gesture of conciliation between the United States and the Six Nations.

ing the Revolution. At General Haldimand's invitation, they settled along the Grand River on a tract of 675,000 acres between Lakes Erie and Ontario. Haldimand, who virtually alone among British officials kept his word to the Indians, had bought the land from the Mississauga Indians to fulfill his wartime pledge to compensate pro-British Iroquois.

Residents of this new Six Nations Reserve soon recreated the structures of the old confederacy. They kindled the central fire in the new home of the Onondaga, revived the council of hereditary chiefs, and even obtained half of the old wampum belts from their New York brethren. The Iroquois were now permanently divided into two confederacies—one in Canada, the other in the United States.

Across the border in New York, meanwhile, the Americans whittled away relentlessly at Iroquois territory. It was not just that most of the Iroquois had been on the wrong side in the war—the Oneida and the Tuscarora fared little better—but that they all were in the way. State officials and private speculators eager to open up new lands applied constant pressure on the chiefs to sign away tribal holdings for a pittance. The Oneida and Tuscarora, the nations farthest east now that the Mohawk had vacated their valley, were the first to feel the encroachments of their erstwhile American allies. In 1785 they ceded 1,600 square miles for $15,500. Then the Onondaga and Cayuga sold off all but a few tracts. Soon only the Onondaga would retain any substantial portion of their homeland—a 6,100-acre reservation south of present-day Syracuse.

The Seneca, largest of the nations, resisted initial attempts to buy their holdings in New York. This region west of the Genesee River contained some four million acres—including not only Seneca communities and hunting grounds but also, at Buffalo Creek, near the site of today's city of Buffalo, several settlements of Cayugas, Onondagas, and Tuscaroras who had taken refuge there. Here, the Iroquois remaining in the United States reestablished the old Grand Council and rekindled the fire.

But land speculators continued to hound the Seneca. Robert Morris, a Philadelphia financier who had helped bankroll the American Revolution, served as the agent for the Holland Land Company. This coalition of Dutch bankers foresaw the fortune to be made in opening the region to white settlement. In the summer of 1797, Morris's son Thomas, substituting for his financially harried father—who was hiding at home to escape creditors—managed to bring the Seneca to the negotiating table. Young Morris manipulated the meeting with consummate skill. After the council of sachems spurned all his offers, he made sure the issue was referred to the warriors and prominent women, as was the Seneca custom in matters of controversy. To win the support of Cornplanter and other war chiefs, as well as Red Jacket, the sachems' principal orator, Morris expanded on the tradition of gift giving and offered what amounted to bribes. He promised Red Jacket—who earlier had denounced the senior Morris as "the great Eater with a big belly endeavoring to devour our lands"—an annuity of $60 for the rest of his life. The women were offered presents of clothing and trinkets, and assured that the money would enable them to hire white men to plow their fields.

For $100,000, the women and warriors sold 95 percent of their territory, all but about 310 square miles. The Treaty of Big Tree reserved for Seneca occupancy seven tiny tracts along the Genesee River and four large ones known by the streams they abutted—Buffalo Creek, Cattaraugus, Allegany, and Tonawanda. (Later, the company ceded two square miles of former Seneca land north of the Tonawanda tract to the landless Tuscarora.) The purchase price at Big Tree was invested in bank stock in the nation's name; the income paid each of the 1,500 or so native residents an annual sum of less than $4.

Solomon O'Bail, Cornplanter's grandson, appears in a late-19th-century photograph in Iroquois dress, including a turkey-feather headdress and a sash—an article the Iroquois customarily wove by hand, using strands of many colors (left). By this time, traditional eagle-feather headdresses had largely been replaced by bonnets of turkey feathers (right), which were easier to obtain and provided a fancier display.

The treaty, ratified by the new American Congress, created the Indian reservation system and imposed a new way of life. The tracts that the Seneca and other Iroquois reserved for their own use—hence, the term reservation—restricted their freedom. Soon their old hunting grounds would be dotted with white farms and settlements. Iroquois men felt a greater jolt than the women, for most men now had lost their callings as warriors and diplomats and long-range hunters. Soon the main occupation open to them would be farming, but that was seen as women's work.

The radical change in social and economic circumstances was recognized by Joseph Brant on one side of the border and Cornplanter on the other. Both saw the need for Iroquois communities to adopt the animal-drawn plow and other farming techniques from the whites and for Iroquois men to undertake such tasks, thus usurping the women's role.

On the new Six Nations Reserve in Canada, where he wielded near-dictatorial power, Brant came up with a novel stratagem for achieving this difficult transition. He encouraged the practice of leasing or selling

land to white farmers, who would then serve as models for the Indians as well as providing income that could be invested in livestock and equipment. In the face of vigorous opposition from Canadian authorities who, unlike their American counterparts, worried that the Indians might be victimized, Brant and his chiefs quickly sold or leased some 350,000 acres—more than half the reservation. By Brant's death in 1807, the scheme had helped many Indians become successful farmers, but it also had created a quagmire of disputed deeds and leases. In fact, so many illegal white squatters took up residence that in order to evict them and preserve the remaining Indian land, the council agreed to surrender the reserve to the government to be held in trust for its Indian residents.

Across the border in the United

States, Cornplanter was the most vigorous Iroquois advocate of learning the white man's skills. He lived with about 400 followers along the Allegheny River—a few miles south of the Seneca's larger Allegany Reservation—on a grant of one square mile given him by the Commonwealth of Pennsylvania for services rendered in land transactions. Cornplanter, who had personally appealed to President George Washington to "teach us to plow and to grind corn," encouraged the missionary endeavors of the Society of Friends in Philadelphia. Unlike other denominations, the Quakers were less interested in gaining converts than in promoting education. In Cornplanter's town of Jenuchshadego, they started a grammar school for teaching English, established a model farm, and taught carpentry, blacksmithing, and other crafts.

Such instruction was imperative for more than vocational reasons. The economic, political, and military decline of the Iroquois combined with their treatment by the Americans, which ranged from condescension to contempt, set the stage for social disintegration. The demoralization was so severe that even among the nominal Iroquois victors of the Revolution, the Oneida, Samuel Kirkland saw all but a few of his parishioners reduced to a "filthy, dirty, nasty" condition. Most of the Iroquois settlements were racked by violent family disputes, suspicions of witchcraft, and chronic alcoholism. By the spring of 1799, demon rum was sparking so much turmoil in Cornplanter's own village that it threatened to subvert the best-laid plans of the Quakers.

Among those prey to strong drink was Cornplanter's half-brother, Ganiodaiyo, or Handsome Lake. At 64, Handsome Lake was a well-known medicine man and sachem who was now bedridden, wasting away from drunkenness and despondency in the cabin of his daughter, who described him as "but yellow skin and dried bones." When he got his hands on whiskey, he would rouse himself long enough to sing sacred songs dealing with death before slumping back into a stupor. On the morning of June 15, 1799, the daughter saw him totter outside and collapse. She summoned friends and relatives to carry him back to bed, but they could find no sign of breathing or a heartbeat. Word raced through the village that Handsome Lake was dead or dying.

About two hours later, however, his eyes opened and his lips moved. "My uncle, are you feeling well?" asked his nephew Blacksnake, who was at his bedside. "Yes," Handsome Lake replied, "I believe myself

A watercolor by 20th-century Seneca artist Ernest Smith depicts Handsome Lake, wampum belt in hand, preaching his code of faith and temperance—known to the Iroquois as the Good Word—at the Tonawanda Reservation longhouse. His teachings became the basis for the Longhouse religion, still practiced by many Iroquois today.

well." He told of a powerful dream in which he had been visited by three men in ceremonial dress, with red paint on their faces and feathered bonnets on their heads, who caught him in their arms as he collapsed and laid him gently on the ground. Handsome Lake described them as angels who had been sent by the Creator with an apocalyptic message. Upon pain of death and destruction, the Iroquois were to give up four evil practices: drinking, witchcraft, magic love potions, and medicine that caused abortion and sterility. He later repeated his vision to the villagers in a council convened by Cornplanter. The Iroquois had long looked to their dreams for inspiration, and Handsome Lake's account struck with the force of revelation. Among those on hand was a Quaker, Henry Simmons, who agreed with the Seneca that the vision was genuine and reported later that he felt "the love of God flowing powerfully among us."

Several weeks later, Handsome Lake was visited in a dream by a fourth angel, whom he likened to the Great Spirit. The angel led him on a harrowing journey through hell and heaven and other ethereal realms. Along the way, Handsome Lake beheld ominous visions of the effect on his people of adopting the white man's ways—a jail stocked with a whip, handcuffs, and a hangman's noose, and a church with no doors or windows, where he could hear the cries of captive worshipers. But even more frightening prospects awaited him in hell, where a monster he called "the punisher" tortured those Indians who had broken the angels' commandments. There drunkards imbibed molten metal, witches stewed in cauldrons, and wife beaters pounded their fists against the image of a woman that glowed red hot and singed the flesh from their bones. When Handsome Lake at last reached heaven, the angel informed him that it was his mission to return to the earth-world and begin preaching the divine message he had been blessed with—the Gaiwiio, or "Good Word."

Handsome Lake was a born evangelist. Indians came from miles away to hear his revelations. Every year, accompanied by a few disciples, he ventured to other reservations and to the Grand Council at Buffalo Creek. Despite his age and recent infirmity, he traveled on foot and preached his gospel with the certitude of a visionary. One who saw the prophet at his peak recalled that he wore a blaze of paint from the corner of each eye and long silver quills on each ear: "On his arms were wide silver bracelets—his leggings were of red cloth and his covering a blanket over all—which he threw off in council and took up his long pipe."

As the prophet's preaching evolved, it became an amalgam of old and new ideas that exerted broad appeal. Handsome Lake borrowed from

A leather bag with glass beads resembling wampum and a moccasin with panels of loom-woven quillwork (bottom) show how native craftswomen put new materials and techniques to traditional uses.

A GENIUS FOR DECORATION

An expanding market for Indian wares in the 1800s allowed women on reservations in New York and nearby Canada to profit by skills they had long used to decorate their own apparel *(above).* Employing colored beads, softened porcupine quills, or dyed moose hair, they embellished various trade articles with exquisite designs. Among those plying the craft were not only Iroquois but Canadian Hurons whose ancestors had escaped destruction or assimilation in the 1600s. Samples of this remarkable handiwork are shown here and on the following pages.

A shell gorget is linked by shoulder straps to trailing quillwork depicting thunderbirds and jagged lightning—a motif the Iroquois and Huron shared with other tribes.

Patches of leather embroidered with dyed moose hair embellish a Huron tobacco pouch fashioned from the hoof of a caribou.

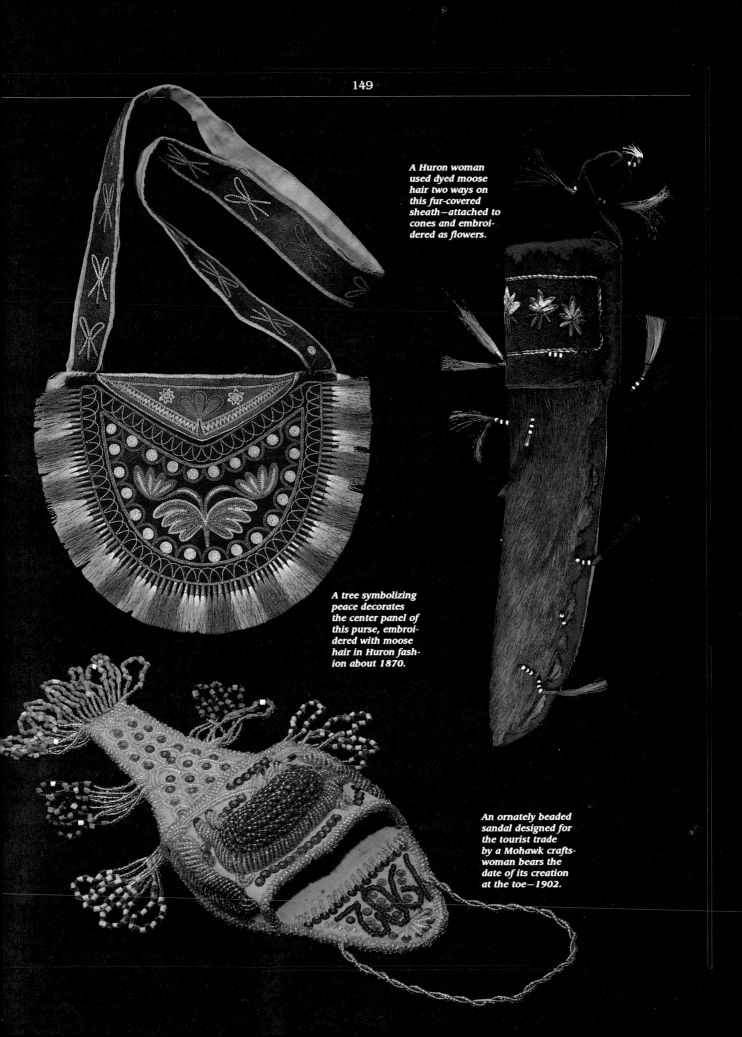

A Huron woman used dyed moose hair two ways on this fur-covered sheath—attached to cones and embroidered as flowers.

A tree symbolizing peace decorates the center panel of this purse, embroidered with moose hair in Huron fashion about 1870.

An ornately beaded sandal designed for the tourist trade by a Mohawk craftswoman bears the date of its creation at the toe—1902.

Hundreds of glass beads of European manufacture went into this kaleidoscopic display of leaves and flowers on a purse of rough fabric, crafted on a reservation in Canada in the 1800s.

The designer of this sash used glass beads to evoke the age-old allure of shell-bead wampum, prized by the Iroquois for its mythical associations.

traditional Iroquois sacred beliefs by encouraging the observance of the annual calendar of festivals. He told his followers, for example, that during his dream journey to heaven he met a white dog he had earlier sacrificed in ancestral fashion to honor the Good Twin and the coming of a new year. It was important to continue such ceremonies, he believed, for the Good Twin, who brought bounty to the faithful, was an incarnation of the Great Spirit. At the same time, Handsome Lake took a leaf from Christianity with his emphasis on eternal punishment for evildoers and redemption for those who repented. All this spoke to the anxieties that gripped the Iroquois at a time of drastic change.

Rival sachems were less enthusiastic about the political power that Handsome Lake and his supporters were beginning to wield. Not long after he began to spread his gospel, Handsome Lake nearly embroiled the Seneca in a war with nearby Delaware Indians. The controversy began when Cornplanter's daughter fell gravely ill after giving birth to a child by a Delaware chief. Consulted in his role as prophet and medicine man, Handsome Lake concluded that the young woman had been bewitched by Delawares—a diagnosis that confirmed the suspicions of villagers, who thought that the sorcerers' motive was to relieve the Delaware chief of the burden of marrying the mother of his child. When the alarmed Delawares sent one of their own medicine men to examine the patient, Senecas took him hostage and said they would kill him if she died—a threat that, if fulfilled, was sure to spark fighting between the two sides.

The explosive issue was taken up by the Grand Council at Buffalo Creek in 1801. The sachems who gathered there were concerned not only with the prospect of war with the Delaware but with the fact that Handsome Lake was beginning to level charges of witchcraft against other prominent Senecas. Among those he denounced was the influential orator Red Jacket, who heatedly defended himself, accusing Handsome Lake of inventing charges of sorcery in league with Cornplanter to augment their power. In the end, Red Jacket escaped condemnation, but the chiefs acknowledged Handsome Lake's authority by appointing him "high priest, and principal sachem of all things civil and religious." As one chief put it, he had been "deputed by the four angels to transact our business." In the aftermath, Cornplanter pledged peace to the Delaware—contrary to expectations, his daughter was clinging to life. But the Delaware were so shaken that the entire community left the area, settling eventually among the Canadian Iroquois at Grand River.

Handsome Lake's new position as supreme leader of the Six Nations

in the United States was unprecedented and precarious, given the traditional reluctance of the Iroquois to be dictated to. Among those who resented his authority were devotees of the false face and other medicine societies—whose rites Handsome Lake abhorred (some of the medicine men had taken to imbibing alcohol for inspiration). When he moved to disband the societies, however, he stirred up fears among the people that illness and misfortune would result. In the end, he was forced to compromise, allowing the rites to continue in conjunction with annual festivals, provided that the society members abstained from strong drink.

Handsome Lake's own solution to the perennial problem of sickness was to continue rooting out suspected witches. One of his visions, he said, had given him a special ability to spot sorcerers. He gave those he accused a chance to confess their sins and thus undo the evil spell, but a

The Logan family gathers in front of its home on the Onondaga Reservation in 1905. Their rough-hewn timber cabin, a style borrowed from English colonists, is typical of the first homes built on the reservation when it was established in 1788. Only a few remain standing today.

few who refused to recant were put to death, much to the dismay of their kin. Resentment grew as illness persisted. Some people blamed Handsome Lake for interfering with tradition and angering the spirits.

Handsome Lake's preoccupation with witches and his tendency to alienate other sachems soon cost him his position as supreme leader of the Six Nations and drove a wedge through his own band of Senecas. In 1803, after a falling out with Cornplanter, he took a group of his followers north to the Allegany Reservation and started a new settlement there called Coldspring. Quakers advised him to disperse his followers across the countryside in independent homesteads as white farmers were doing, but he felt it imperative to keep the people together in a village center for ceremonial purposes. His utopian vision of a community held together by rituals and respect for divine law was soon dispelled, however. An epidemic in 1807 led to renewed witch hunts—and fresh suspicions that Handsome Lake was exceeding his rightful authority and compounding the miseries of his people. One of his Coldspring followers, his nephew Henry O'Bail, broke with him publicly, denying the very existence of witchcraft. In 1809 Handsome Lake pulled up stakes and moved on with a few followers to the Tonawanda Reservation.

What remained of his political strength was expended in 1812 when he preached against Iroquois participation in the renewal of hostilities between the United States and Great Britain. Handsome Lake was no foe of the government in Washington—a decade earlier he had called on President Thomas Jefferson, who praised the Seneca leader as an instrument of change for his people. But Handsome Lake saw himself as a prophet of peace and resisted American efforts to counter the British recruitment of Mohawks in Canada by soliciting volunteers among the New York Iroquois. His stern opposition proved effective only on the Allegany and Tonawanda reservations. More than 600 Iroquois from other reservations, including Handsome Lake's nephew and chief disciple, Blacksnake, heeded the call from Washington to fight in defense of what many of the Indians now referred to as "our country."

Like other visionaries of his time, Handsome Lake had faltered as a political leader, in part through overzealousness. But he exerted a profound and lasting influence on his people. His preaching amounted to a social gospel that called on the Iroquois to amend their ways without losing pride in their past. He recognized that to survive, the Iroquois would require families as strong as their clans had once been. To that end, he railed against drunkenness, debauchery, easy divorce, and the practice of

abortion. And he sought to give Iroquois men a new stake in domestic life by holding them responsible for the economic well-being of the family and by denouncing some of the traditional prerogatives of women, such as a mother's right to interfere in her daughter's marriage.

By the time Handsome Lake died in 1815, after repeated visions of his approaching death and a 150-mile journey on foot to the Onondaga Reservation, his gospel had galvanized the Iroquois. Many of them had stopped drinking; by one estimate, three-fourths of the Seneca Nation now espoused temperance. With his own Allegany band as the spearhead, the movement to embrace white farming technology while retaining the old Iroquois sense of community was spreading rapidly. Senecas and others split rails for fences, built houses and barns, laid roads, plowed fields, tended livestock, and set up shop as blacksmiths, carpenters, and other providers of skills essential to an agricultural economy.

Disciples continued to spread the prophet's teachings. Largely through the work of his grandson, Jimmy Johnson, his message was preserved in the oral tradition known as the Code of Handsome Lake, which

Pupils approach the Seneca Mission School on the Buffalo Creek Reservation near Niagara Falls, in an 1821 drawing by Dennis Cusick, one of the displaced Tuscaroras who joined the Senecas at Buffalo Creek in the early 1800s. Mission schools sought to convert the Indians not only to Christianity but also to the white settlers' way of life.

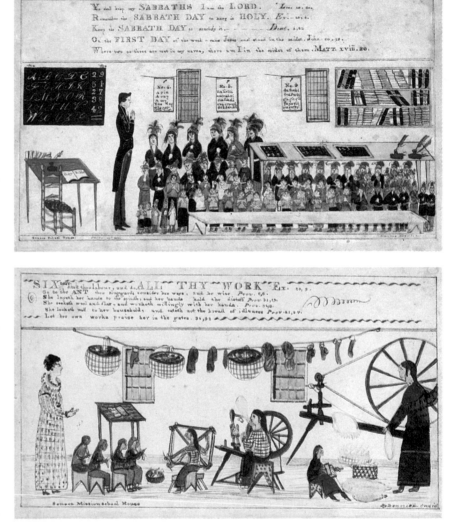

A Cusick drawing framed by Bible verses portrays mission teacher James Young leading a class on the Buffalo Creek Reservation. On the wall hang examples of written English for the Seneca students to follow.

James Young's wife teaches carding, spinning, and knitting to Iroquois girls in another Cusick drawing. In addition to reading and writing, missionaries taught what they referred to as "the arts of civilization"— agricultural subjects for the boys and domestic ones for the girls.

became the foundation for a movement called the Old Way of Handsome Lake, or simply the Longhouse religion, because the biennial ceremonies in which the code was recited took place in buildings modeled after that traditional structure. The code bound together scattered remnants of the Six Nations on both sides of the border. From the mid-19th century on, about one-fourth of all Iroquois followed the Old Way of Handsome Lake—the prophet who had risen from drunkenness and despair to help revitalize his people.

Even during the spiritual renaissance initiated by Handsome Lake, the Iroquois faced new threats to their survival as a people. The prophet had inveighed against the sale of additional lands, but members of the Six Nations continued to scatter as white settlements encircled their reservations and the pressure to sell mounted. As early as 1807, the Cayuga had ceded their last two small reservations to the state of New York. Many of them immigrated to the Sandusky River in northern Ohio along with other Iroquois, while the rest took up residence on Seneca reservations. Then in 1831, after the federal government began urging Indians to migrate west of the Mississippi to open up their lands to white settlement, these Cayugas and other Iroquois swapped their Ohio holdings for a reservation in what is now northeastern Oklahoma.

Many Oneidas also sold out and headed west. After the death of Samuel Kirkland in 1808, they had come under the influence of another clergyman, the Reverend Eleazar Williams. Born of Iroquois parents in the mostly Mohawk community of Caughnawaga, Williams was a spellbinding speaker who converted many of his fellow Indians to the Episcopalian faith. He dreamed of using his converts to establish a church-based Iroquois community in the West. Despite opposition from much of the nation, he engineered the sale of part of its New York holdings and purchased a large tract near Green Bay, Wisconsin. In 1823 he and 600 Oneidas settled there. Some 400 of the Oneidas remaining in New York elected to relocate to Ontario two decades later.

The pressure to sell was greatest on the Seneca, for they were the only Iroquois nation that still occupied large areas of fertile land in western New York. Speculators of the Ogden Land Company, which had purchased negotiation rights from the Dutch bankers, chipped away at the Seneca holdings. In 1826 company agents purchased the remaining small tracts along the Genesee River and sizable portions of three of the four major reservations. In 1838, with the Treaty of Buffalo Creek, the company nearly succeeded in swindling the Indians out of everything that remained. Using chicanery, they obtained the signatures of a bare majority of Seneca leaders on a treaty ceding every last remaining acre. The purchase price totaled $202,000, or one-tenth of the appraised value of $2,000,000. More than 2,000 Senecas, together with several hundred other Iroquois still living in New York, were to take up new homes in Kansas, where they presumably would be out of the white man's way.

The circumstances surrounding the treaty were so blatantly corrupt that most Senecas refused to support it. Their protests and the public alarms raised by the Quakers and the Reverend Asher Wright, a Protestant missionary at Buffalo Creek, forced the Ogden Company to reconsider. In 1842 the company agreed to a compromise that allowed the Seneca to retain two of the four reservations—Cattaraugus and Allegany. Residents of a third, Tonawanda, protested that they had not been a party to the new treaty and launched a long legal fight that would eventually reach the Supreme Court. Meanwhile, some occupants of the disbanded Buffalo Creek Reservation joined a group of 215 Indians who departed in 1846 for the frontier destination originally intended for all the New York Indians. Many fell ill and died in Kansas; one-third of the original party went back home the following year, complaining of the climate and of the hostility of the Indians already living there.

Those who returned to the Allegany and Cattaraugus reservations were caught up in a revolution. Faith in the leadership there had been so undermined by the land-sale scandal and other instances of corruption that in 1848 a convention of Senecas from the two reservations staged a

Transplanted Mohawks from the Akwe-sasane Reservation arrive in Lawrence, Kansas, in 1894 to market their wares. Most of the Iroquois who were forced west during the land scandals of the mid-1800s perished or returned to New York; the few who remained in Kansas sustained themselves in part by selling baskets and other crafts.

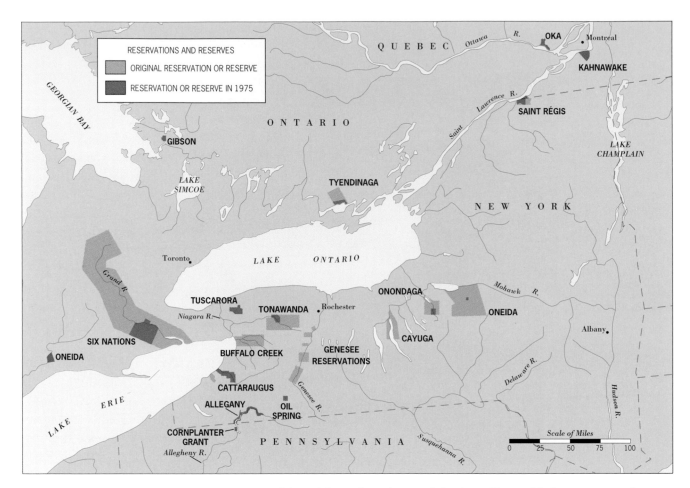

RESERVATIONS AND RESERVES
- ORIGINAL RESERVATION OR RESERVE
- RESERVATION OR RESERVE IN 1975

As shown above, a series of outright property seizures and questionable land deals have confined the Iroquois to a few small reservations in Canada—where many Mohawks and members of the other nations fled about the time of the American Revolution—and scattered tracts in New York State, where the Iroquois once held undisputed mastery.

peaceful uprising. They deposed the hereditary chiefs—a process known as dehorning, since the chiefs traditionally had worn antler headdresses—and replaced them with a council to be elected annually. A written constitution was adopted, and the Allegany and Cattaraugus reservations formally banded together as the Seneca Nation.

The desire for democracy eventually spread to the Six Nations Reserve in Canada, where the Dehorners would ultimately prevail. But in New York, at the Onondaga Reservation—which had again become home to the council fire after the sale of Buffalo Creek—power remained in the hands of hereditary chiefs, as it did among the Tonawanda Seneca, who were preoccupied with their struggle to reclaim their reservation. In 1857 the Tonawanda won a historic concession from the Supreme Court—the right to repurchase just over half of the land they had been cheated out of in 1838, using money originally set aside for their removal to Kansas.

One of their hereditary sachems and a leader in the long legal fight was a remarkable young man named Ely Samuel Parker. A descendant of Handsome Lake, Cornplanter, and Red Jacket, Parker began his rise in 1844 as a 16-year-old interpreter for his people in negotiations at the state capital of Albany. That same year, Parker had a chance encounter in an Albany bookstore with a Rochester attorney named Lewis Henry Morgan. Morgan was so fascinated by the Iroquois that in college he had formed a fraternal organization modeled after the confederacy. Like other Americans before him, including Benjamin Franklin, he regarded the Iroquois confederacy as an inspiration for the American union. After meeting Parker, Morgan enlisted the young Seneca as his interpreter and collaborator and produced in 1851 the first scientific study of American Indians, *The League of the Iroquois*. This classic established Morgan as a pioneer of American anthropology and brought a new appreciation for the traditions of the Iroquois.

The book also helped launch Parker on a meteoric career. He studied law, but because Indians lacked citizenship, he did not qualify for the New York bar and took up civil engineering in the employ of the federal government. After the Civil War erupted, he became one of many New York Indians to enlist in the Union army. He rose to the rank of brigadier general and served as military secretary to General Ulysses S. Grant. In that capacity, Parker transcribed the surrender terms signed by General Robert E. Lee at Appomattox Court House in 1865. (Lee at first seemed startled by Parker's appearance, but then extended his hand and said, "I am glad to see one real American here.") Four years later, after Grant was elected president, he named Parker commissioner of Indian affairs, the first Native American to serve in that post.

Although a number of Iroquois would follow Parker's example and

Reflecting their claim to sovereignty, many Iroquois carry passports issued by the Six Nations Reserve in Canada. The passports, bearing instructions in French, English, and Iroquois, are recognized by 36 nations around the world, not including the United States. Embossed on the cover is the Tree of Peace—symbol of the perennial accord between the Iroquois nations—encircled by clan emblems, including the turtle, bear, deer, and beaver.

achieve success in the white man's world, the longing for independence remained strong. As Indian tribes across the continent were confined to reservations, many Iroquois continued to assert their ancient claim to sovereignty. Citing old treaties signed in the wake of the American Revolution, they insisted that they were not subject to the laws of either the United States or Canada. This campaign took many forms. Various Iroquois councils issued their own declarations of war against Germany during World War I, tried to deny the right of Congress to grant them American citizenship in 1924, and protested against the draft during World War II—although many Iroquois served with distinction in both the American and the Canadian armed forces. In a rare legal concession in the late 1920s, federal courts upheld the right of unrestricted free passage for Iroquois across the United States-Canada border. Several decades later, Canadian Iroquois of the Six Nations Reserve would begin issuing their own passports for travel to other destinations.

Preserving the time-honored custom of ceremonial dancing, couples adorned with colorful beadwork circle the floor arm in arm at an Iroquois festival in New York.

Two of the most forceful advocates of Iroquois sovereignty during the first half of the 20th century were women. The traditional power of Iroquois women had been eclipsed during the previous century by the emergence of male authority within the home and of governing councils made up of elected members rather than hereditary chiefs chosen by tribal matriarchs. But with the rise to prominence of Laura Cornelius Kellogg and Alice Lee Jemison, Iroquois women stepped again from the political shadows. Kellogg was born to a prominent family in the Wisconsin branch of the Oneida and received a college education, while Jemison grew up poor among the Seneca on the Cattaraugus Reservation and had to forgo her plans to attend college and law school and make her way as a freelance journalist and legal researcher. Yet both waged tireless struggles to correct what they saw as injustices.

Kellogg, together with her husband, a white lawyer, set up headquarters at Onondaga and pursued a class-action suit demanding the return of 18 million acres of land that had been taken from the Six Nations under various pretenses since the American Revolution. Jemison lobbied for the Seneca Nation in Washington, D.C., where she led a crusade to abolish the Bureau of Indian Affairs, under the slogan The Only Good Bureau Is a Dead Bureau. Both women faced criticism of their tactics, and neither succeeded in her ultimate goal, but they kept alive the spirit of Iroquois resistance to federal intrusions.

During the second half of the 20th century, the Iroquois not only failed to regain lost territories but were required to forfeit additional lands. The fact that the rationale was public improvements was little solace for those affected. In spite of their protests, the Mohawk lost territory on both sides of the border to the construction of the Saint Lawrence Seaway. The Tuscarora, for their part, took the New York State Power Authority to court after it claimed a sizable piece of their reservation for a hydroelectric project along the Niagara River. When the state began construction work while the case was still under consideration, Tuscaroras lay down in front of the bulldozers. The amount of land claimed was ultimately reduced, and their determination sparked a new militancy among the Iroquois. Senecas at the Allegany Reservation challenged the right of the U. S. Army Corps of Engineers to build a dam on the Allegheny River that would inundate 9,000 acres of their territory, including the village where Handsome Lake had received his visions. Their case appeared strong, for the Canandaigua Treaty of 1794 stated that "the United States acknowledges all the land within the aforementioned boundaries, to be the property of the Seneca Nation, and the United States will never claim the same, nor disturb the Seneca Nation." Yet in 1959, the Supreme Court refused to hear their appeal, and the birthplace of the Longhouse religion vanished beneath the waters.

Despite such disheartening setbacks, the Iroquois sense of sovereignty has endured. Even those who labor in cities far from their ancestral homes—like the Mohawk ironworkers who brave heights to build bridges and skyscrapers—are bound by feelings of national pride and solidarity. Today, the descendants of the old confederacy are dispersed across North America, covering a distance of nearly 2,000 miles and encompassing 16 different reservations in New York, Wisconsin, Oklahoma, Ontario, and Quebec. But they share a conviction that theirs was the first union of American states, and that spirit persists whenever Iroquois come together to honor their traditions of peace and power. ◆

HIGH STEEL MOHAWKS

A Mohawk iron-worker surveys a city from a precarious perch in a painting by Onondaga artist Arnold Jacobs. He painted the work as a tribute to his Mohawk brother-in-law who died in a fall and to all other Indian ironworkers claimed by accidents. Jacobs explained that the eagle hovering behind the worker represents the freedom that men feel when they work up high, without walls.

"When they talk about the men that built this country, one of the men they mean is me," stated Orvis Diabo proudly in 1949. Like thousands of other Mohawks, Diabo earned his living as an ironworker, erecting bridges and skyscrapers in 17 states.

The story of Mohawk ironworkers began in 1886 when the Canadian Pacific Railroad built a bridge across the Saint Lawrence River near Montreal. The south abutment of the span rested on Mohawk land at the Caughnawaga (Kahnawake) Reservation. To obtain permission to build there, the Dominion Bridge Company agreed to hire Indians for the job. The results were more than satisfactory. As one Dominion official later described it, "Putting riveting tools in the Mohawk's hands was like putting ham with eggs. They were natural-born bridgemen."

Their reputation spread, and within the year, 50 Mohawks were hired to help build the Sault Sainte Marie Bridge in northern Michigan. The wages were good, but the work was perilous, as one Mohawk fell to his death on the project. Scores of other Indians died in their first decades of ironworking, including 33 who were killed in 1907 in the collapse of Quebec Bridge.

Undeterred, Mohawks continued in the trade and made the transition from constructing bridges to erecting skyscrapers when a building boom hit New York City in the early 20th century. Mohawks helped erect almost all of New York's giant towers, including the RCA Building, Rockefeller Center, and the quarter-mile-high Empire State Building. By 1957 there were about 800 Mohawks living and working in the city. So many settled in the north Gowanus section of Brooklyn that the neighborhood came to be known as "Downtown Caughnawaga."

Today, a new generation of Mohawks and other Iroquois maintains the tradition, working on high steel across the country and taking pride in mastering a difficult and dangerous profession. Some say these Indian crews echo the ways of their warrior ancestors who traveled across the Northeast in brotherly bands, seeking adventure and earning respect. But Leroy Ferguson, a modern Mohawk, explains it more succinctly: Indians have an affinity for high steel, he says, because "they are not afraid to die."

COWBOYS OF THE SKY

All early-20th-century ironworkers faced tremendous dangers in the days before mandatory safety regulations; approximately 2,000 were killed on the job between 1900 and 1920. Of all the accidents that occurred in those early years, however, none matched the great Quebec Bridge disaster.

At 5:37 p.m. on August 29, 1907, men working on the Quebec Bridge nine miles above Quebec City heard rivets start to pop and felt enormous steel girders twist beneath them. Ninety-six men died when the span crashed into the Saint Lawrence River, 33 of whom were Mohawks from the Caughnawaga Reservation. The exact cause of the catastrophe is unknown, but it may have been related to a damaged shipment of steel. Among the Mohawk people, this is still spoken of as "the disaster."

"People thought the disaster would scare the Indians away from high steel for good," said one Mohawk ironworker. "Instead, it made high steel much more interesting to them. It made them take pride in themselves that they could do such dangerous work."

Late-19th-century Mohawk ironworkers gather on a partially constructed bridge. Called "cowboys of the sky," these daring men lived exciting, but often short, lives. In 1890 ironworking had the highest mortality rate in the construction trade.

One arm of the Quebec Bridge stretches above the Saint Lawrence River in a photograph taken on August 28, 1907, one day before the span collapsed. At 1,800 feet, the structure was conceived as the longest cantilever bridge of its kind in the world.

An iron cross was erected on the Caughnawaga Reservation to serve as a memorial to the large number of Mohawk ironworkers killed on the job.

One day after the Quebec Bridge tragedy, twisted rubble from the collapsed span covers the bank of the Saint Lawrence River. Nine years later, the ill-fated bridge was being rebuilt by another firm when the center span collapsed, killing 60 to 70 more bridgemen.

CHASING THE BOOM

In the 1920s, crews of Mohawk iron-workers traveled from Caughnawaga to New York City, lured there by a building boom and promises of high wages. These men helped shape the distinctive skyline of the city, working on the George Washington Bridge, the Chrysler Building, and many other modern structures. As the reputation of Mohawk ironworkers grew, other members of the Iroquois Nation joined the profession and established them-selves on crews across the land.

New York City iron-workers, including Mohawks, take a lunch break some 70 stories above the city on a girder of the RCA Building in 1928. "You don't pay much attention to how tall a build-ing is," explained Tom Lahache, an experienced Mo-hawk iron man. "If you slip, 50 feet is as bad as 500 feet."

Mohawk riveter Jo-seph Jocks works on San Francisco's Golden Gate Bridge, completed in 1937. Mohawks were will-ing to travel to vir-tually any urban center in the United States or Canada in order to find jobs and adventures.

Mohawk ironworkers Joseph Albaney (left) and Pepper Martin celebrate the completion of the Rainbow Bridge over Niagara Falls in 1941 by exchanging Canadian and American flags.

Hundreds of feet above midtown Manhattan, iron-workers of Mohawk descent work on the 54-story Equitable Life Assurance Building, completed in 1985. Like most high steel workers, these Mohawks shun protective ropes and harnesses, claiming that they limit freedom of movement.

ACKNOWLEDGMENTS

The editors wish to thank the following individuals and institutions for their valuable assistance:
In Canada: Ontario—Patricia Hess, The Woodland Cultural Centre, Brantford. Quebec—Margot Reid, Canadian Museum of Civilization, Hull.
In Denmark: Copenhagen—Berete Due, Nationalmuseet, Etnografisk Samling.

In England: London—J. Hamill.
In France: Aisne—Sylvie Péharpré, Musée National de la Coopération Franco-Américaine, Château de Blérancourt.
In the United States:
Maryland: Baltimore—Donald T. Fritz, The Lacrosse Hall of Fame Museum.
New York: Albany—Lisa Anderson, George Hamell, The New York State Museum. Apalachin—Delores Elliot, Otsiningo American Indian Program. Howes Cave—Christina B. Johannsen, Stephanie Shultes, Iroquois Indian Museum. Liverpool—Valerie Bell, Ste. Marie Among the Iroquois, Onondaga Lake Park. Rochester—Leatrice Kemp, Betty Prisch, Rochester Museum and Science Center. Sanborn—The Iroquois Nationals Board of Directors.
Washington, D.C.: Felicia Pickering, Museum of Natural History, Smithsonian Institution.

PICTURE CREDITS

The sources for the illustrations that appear in this book are listed below. Credits from left to right are separated by semicolons; from top to bottom they are separated by dashes.

Cover: Photo by Arnaud Carpentier, Connaissance des Arts, Paris/courtesy the Trustees of the National Museums of Scotland, Edinburgh. **6, 7:** Library of Congress; art by Karen Barnes of Wood, Ronsaville, Harlin, Inc. **8, 9:** © J. Schwabel, Panoramic Images, Chicago; Dean R. Snow; art by Karen Barnes of Wood, Ronsaville, Harlin, Inc. **10, 11:** Art by Karen Barnes of Wood, Ronsaville, Harlin, Inc.; © Carr Clifton. **12, 13:** © J. Schwabel, Panoramic Images, Chicago; art by Karen Barnes of Wood, Ronsaville, Harlin, Inc. **14, 15:** © Carr Clifton; © J. Schwabel, Panoramic Images, Chicago; art by Karen Barnes of Wood, Ronsaville, Harlin, Inc. **16, 17:** Art by Karen Barnes of Wood, Ronsaville, Harlin, Inc.; © J. Schwabel, Panoramic Images, Chicago. **18, 19:** © Carr Clifton; © J. Schwabel, Panoramic Images, Chicago; art by Karen Barnes of Wood, Ronsaville, Harlin, Inc. **20:** Rochester Museum and Science Center. **22, 23:** Bibliothèque Nationale, Paris. **24:** Map by Maryland CartoGraphics, Inc. **25:** New York State Museum. **26:** Photo by Pamela Dewey, courtesy National Museum of the American Indian, Smithsonian Institution, Washington, D.C., no. 14/3269. **28:** New York State Museum. **29:** The Granger Collection. **31:** Photo by Karen Furth, courtesy National Museum of the American Indian, Smithsonian Institution, Washington, D.C., no. 2/2790. **32:** Rochester Museum and Science Center. **33:** National Museum of the American Indian, Smithsonian Institution, Washington, D.C., no. 15289. **34, 35:** Jean-Loup Charmet, Paris, Archives Nationales Musée. **37:** Peabody Museum, Harvard University, photo by Hillel Burger, photo no. T904; Richard Hill. **39:** Tuscarora, painting by Wilfred Chew. **40:** Woodland Cultural Centre; Richard Hill. **41:** Private Collection. **42:** Rochester Museum and Science Center. **44:** National Museum of the American Indian, Smithsonian Institution, Washington, D.C., no. 15337. **45:** Smithsonian Institution, Washington, D.C., no. 81-2619. **46:** Richard Hill. **48, 49:** Peabody Museum of Natural History, Yale University—Smithsonian Institution, Washington, D.C., no. 80-16635—The National Museum of Denmark, Department of Ethnography, Copenhagen, photographed by Kit Weiss (4). **51:** Rare Books and Manu-

scripts Division, The New York Public Library, Astor, Lenox and Tilden Foundations. **52:** Copyright British Museum, London. **54:** Rare Books and Manuscripts Division, The New York Public Library, Astor, Lenox and Tilden Foundations. **56, 57:** © The Detroit Institute of Arts, Cranbrook Institute of Science, © Robert Hensleigh, photographer. **58, 59:** Art by Rob Wood of Wood, Ronsaville, Harlin, Inc. **60, 61:** Inset National Museum of the American Indian, Smithsonian Institution, Washington, D.C., cat. no. 2489; art by Rob Wood of Wood, Ronsaville, Harlin, Inc. **62, 63:** Inset The National Museum of Denmark, Department of Ethnography, Copenhagen, photographed by Kit Weiss; art by Rob Wood of Wood, Ronsaville, Harlin, Inc. **64, 65:** Insets New York State Museum; art by Rob Wood of Wood, Ronsaville, Harlin, Inc. **66, 67:** Photo by Karen Furth, courtesy National Museum of the American Indian, Smithsonian Institution, Washington, D.C., nos. 13/2890-2, 13/2902,3,7, 21/6222; New York State Museum. **68:** Canadian Museum of Civilization, Hull, Quebec, photographed by Richard Garner; New York State Museum. **69:** Smithsonian Institution, Washington, D.C., no. 93-2051—Rochester Museum and Science Center. **70, 71:** © Justin Kerr—photo by E. Fiévet, Chartres; Smithsonian Institution, Washington, D.C., no. 93-2048; courtesy of Glenbow, Calgary, Alberta/Museum of Anthropology and Ethnography, Saint Petersburg, Russia. **72, 73:** Inset Woodland Cultural Centre; New York State Museum (2); Collection Musée de l'Homme, Cl. M. Delaplanche. **74, 75:** New York State Museum; Richard Hill—Woodland Cultural Centre. **76:** Léonard de Selva-Tapabor. **78:** Maps by Maryland CartoGraphics, Inc. **82, 83:** Museum of the Fur Trade, except beaver, Bibliothèque Nationale, Paris. **85:** Gianni Dagli Orti, Paris. **86:** Library of Congress, USZ62-60373. **87:** Lauros-Giraudon, Bibliothèque Nationale, Paris. **88:** Copyright British Museum, London; New York State Museum. **89:** New York State Museum. **90:** C. M. Dixon, Canterbury, Kent. **91:** New York State Museum. **93:** Jean-Loup Charmet, Paris. **95:** The Granger Collection. **96:** Courtesy Kateri Center, Mission Saint-Francois-Xavier, Kahnawake, Ontario. **97:** Copyright British Museum, London. **98:** The Granger Collection. **99:** Kanien'kehaka Raotitiohkwa Cultural Center. **100, 101:** Royal Ontario Museum. **103-105:** Rochester Museum and Science Center. **106:** Copyright British Museum, London. **108, 109:** Onondaga Historical Association, Syracuse, New York. **110:** British Library, London. **113:** Larry Sherer, courtesy

The Lacrosse Foundation and Hall of Fame Museum. **114, 115:** Giraudon, Paris/Art Resource, New York. **116, 117:** The National Museum of Denmark, Department of Ethnography, Copenhagen, photographed by Kit Weiss—New York State Museum—Notman Photographic Archives, McCord Museum of Canadian History, Montreal—The Mansell Collection, London. **118, 119:** Larry Sherer, courtesy The Lacrosse Foundation and Hall of Fame Museum; The Lacrosse Foundation and Hall of Fame Museum; Barry J. Pavelec. **120, 121:** Western Australian Newspapers Limited; courtesy Iroquois Nationals Board of Directors (2). **122:** National Gallery of Canada, Ottawa/Transfer from the Canadian War Memorials, 1921. **125:** Dean R. Snow. **126, 127:** Albany Institute of History and Art; © National Gallery of Art. **128:** Map by Maryland CartoGraphics, Inc. **130, 131:** Gianni Dagli Orti, Paris. **132:** Rochester Museum and Science Center. **134:** Library of Congress. **136, 137:** Rochester Museum and Science Center. **138, 139:** Copyright British Museum, London; Library of Congress, USZ62-3811. **140:** Eliot Elisofon for LIFE, courtesy Gilcrease Institute. **141:** Buffalo and Erie County Historical Society. **142:** Peabody Museum, Harvard University, photo by Hillel Burger, photo no. T1227; Buffalo and Erie County Historical Society. **143:** The National Museum of Denmark, Department of Ethnography, Copenhagen, photographed by Kit Weiss. **144, 145:** Rochester Museum and Science Center. **147:** Buffalo and Erie County Historical Society; copyright British Museum, London (2). **148:** Copyright British Museum, London. **149:** The National Museum of Denmark, Department of Ethnography, Copenhagen, photographed by Kit Weiss—copyright British Museum, London (2). **150:** Collection Musée de l'Homme, Cl. M. Delaplanche; copyright British Museum, London. **152:** Courtesy Ste. Marie Among the Iroquois Living History Museum, Onondaga County Parks, Wolcott Collection. **154, 155:** Iroquois Indian Museum, Howes Cave, New York. **156, 157:** Library of Congress, USZ62-42816. **158:** Map by Maryland CartoGraphics, Inc. **159:** Ronnie Farley. **160:** Iroquois Indian Museum, Howes Cave, New York. **162, 163:** Arnold Jacobs, photographed by Rose-Le Studio, Ltd. **164, 165:** National Archives of Canada, PA 29229—Kanien'kehaka Raotitiohkwa Cultural Center; Richard Hill—National Archives of Canada, C9766. **166, 167:** Kanien'kehaka Raotitiohkwa Cultural Center; Bethlehem Steel Corporation—Niagara Falls Public Library. **168, 169:** Catherine Leroy/Sipa Press.

BIBLIOGRAPHY

BOOKS

Abler, Thomas S., ed., *Chainbreaker: The Revolutionary War Memoirs of Governor Blacksnake as Told to Benjamin Williams.* Lincoln: University of Nebraska Press, 1989.

Armstrong, William H., *Warrior in Two Camps: Ely S. Parker, Union General and Seneca Chief.* Syracuse, N.Y.: Syracuse University Press, 1978.

Bonvillain, Nancy, *The Mohawk.* New York: Chelsea House Publishers, 1992.

Bowden, Henry Warner, *American Indians and Christian Missions: Studies in Cultural Conflict.* Chicago: University of Chicago Press, 1981.

Calloway, Colin G., *Crown and Calumet: British-Indian Relations, 1783-1815.* Norman: University of Oklahoma Press, 1987.

Collaer, Paul, *Music of the Americas: An Illustrated Music Ethnology of the Eskimo and American Indian Peoples.* New York: Praeger Publishers, 1970.

Cork, Ella, *The Worst of the Bargain.* San Jacinto, Calif.: Foundation for Social Research, 1962.

Culin, Stewart, *Games of the North American Indians.* New York: Dover Publications, 1975.

Fenton, William N., *The False Faces of the Iroquois.* Norman: University of Oklahoma Press, 1987.

Gehring, Charles T., and William A. Starna, eds. and transls., *A Journey into Mohawk and Oneida Country, 1634-1635: The Journal of Harmen Meyndertsz van den Bogaert.* Syracuse, N.Y.: Syracuse University Press, 1988.

Graymont, Barbara:
The Iroquois. New York: Chelsea House Publishers, 1988.
The Iroquois in the American Revolution. Syracuse, N.Y.: Syracuse University Press, 1972.

Hauptman, Laurence M.:
The Iroquois and the New Deal. Syracuse, N.Y.: Syracuse University Press, 1981.
The Iroquois Struggle for Survival: World War II to Red Power. Syracuse, N.Y.: Syracuse University Press, 1986.

Hertzberg, Hazel W., *The Great Tree and the Longhouse: The Culture of the Iroquois.* New York: Macmillan, 1966.

Hirschfelder, Arlene, and Paulette Molin, *The Encyclopedia of Native American Religions: An Introduction.* New York: Facts On File, 1992.

Jennings, Francis, *The Ambiguous Iroquois Empire: The Covenant Chain Confederation of Indian Tribes with English Colonies from its Beginnings to the Lancaster Treaty of 1744.* New York: W. W. Norton, 1984.

Jennings, Francis, ed., *The History and Culture of Iroquois Diplomacy: An Interdisciplinary Guide to the Treaties of the Six Nations and Their League.* Syracuse, N.Y.: Syracuse University Press, 1985.

Kenton, Edna, ed., *The Jesuit Relations and Allied Documents: Travels and Explorations of the Jesuit Missionaries in North America (1610-1791).* New York: Albert & Charles Boni, 1925.

Morgan, Lewis H.:
League of the Ho-de'-no-sau-nee, Iroquois. Rochester, N.Y.: Sage & Brother, 1851.
League of the Iroquois. New York: Corinth Books, 1962.

Oxendine, Joseph B., *American Indian Sports Heritage.* Champaign, Ill.: Human Kinetics Books, 1988.

Parker, Arthur C.:
The Life of General Ely S. Parker: Last Grand Sachem of the Iroquois and General Grant's Military Secretary. Buffalo: Buffalo Historical Society, 1985.
Parker on the Iroquois. Ed. by William N. Fenton. Syracuse, N.Y.: Syracuse University Press, 1975.

Richter, Daniel K., *The Ordeal of the Longhouse: The Peoples of the Iroquois League in the Era of European Colonization.* Chapel Hill, N.C.: University of North Carolina Press, 1992.

Richter, Daniel K., and James H. Merrell, eds., *Beyond the Covenant Chain: The Iroquois and Their Neighbors in Indian North America, 1600-1800.* Syracuse, N.Y.: Syracuse University Press, 1987.

Ritchie, William A., and Robert E. Funk, *Aboriginal Settlement Patterns in the Northeast.* Albany: University of the State of New York, 1973.

Seaver, James Everett, *A Narrative of the Life of Mary Jemison, the White Woman of the Genesee.* Rev. by Charles Delamater Vail. New York: American Scenic & Historic Preservation Society, 1918.

Speck, Frank Gouldsmith, *The Iroquois: A Study in Cultural Evolution.* Bloomfield Hills, Mich.: Cranbrook Institute of Science, 1982.

The Spirit Sings: Artistic Traditions of Canada's First Peoples. Toronto: McClelland and Stewart, 1987.

Tanner, Helen Hornbeck, ed., *Atlas of Great Lakes Indian History.* Norman: University of Oklahoma Press, 1987.

Trigger, Bruce G.:
The Children of Aataentsic: A History of the Huron People to 1660. Kingston, Ontario: McGill-Queen's University Press, 1987.
The Huron: Farmers of the North. New York: Holt, Rinehart and Winston, 1969.
Natives and Newcomers: Canada's "Heroic Age" Reconsidered. Kingston, Ontario: McGill-Queen's University Press, 1985.

Trigger, Bruce G., ed., *Northeast.* Vol. 15 of *Handbook of North American Indians.* Washington, D.C.: Smithsonian Institution, 1978.

Wallace, Anthony F. C., *The Death and Rebirth of the Seneca.* New York: Alfred A. Knopf, 1970.

Wallace, Paul A. W., *The White Roots of Peace.* Philadelphia: University of Pennsylvania Press, 1946.

Weyand, Alexander M., and Milton R. Roberts, *The Lacrosse Story.* Baltimore: Garamond/Pridemark Press, 1965.

Wilson, Edmund, *Apologies to the Iroquois.* New York: Farrar, Straus and Cudahy, 1960.

PERIODICALS

Blanchard, David, "High Steel! The Kahnawake Mohawk and the High Construction Trade," *The Journal of Ethnic Studies,* Summer 1983.

Brady, Erik, "Indians Carry Flag into Competition," *USA Today,* July 5, 1990.

Conly, Robert L., and B. Anthony Stewart, "The Mohawks Scrape the Sky," *The National Geographic Magazine,* July 1952.

Eyman, Frances, "Lacrosse and the Cayuga Thunder Rite," *Expedition,* Summer 1964.

King, J. C. H., "Woodlands Artifacts from the Studio of Benjamin West 1738-1820," *American Indian Art Magazine,* Winter 1991.

Lipsyte, Robert:
"A Goalie Keeps Faith for an Iroquois Nation," *The New York Times,* January 29, 1993.
"Another National Team, Another Sort of Dream," *The New York Times,* July 31, 1992.

Mitchell, Joseph, "The Mohawks in High Steel," *The New Yorker,* September 17, 1949.

"Showing of Pride for the Iroquois," *The New York Times,* July 16, 1990.

Wray, Charles F., "Ornamental Hair Combs of the Seneca Iroquois," *Pennsylvania Archaeology,* July 1963.

OTHER PUBLICATIONS

Akicita: Early Plains and Woodlands Indian Art from the Collection of Alexander Acevedo. Los Angeles: The Southwest Museum, 1983.

Art from Ganondagan. Waterford: New York State Office of Parks, Recreation and Historic Preservation, 1986.

Council Fire: A Resource Guide. Brantford, Ontario: Woodland Cultural Centre, 1989.

Fredrickson, N. Jaye, and Sandra Gibb, *The Covenant Chain: Indian Ceremonial and Trade Silver.* Ottawa: National Museums of Canada, 1980.

Hill, Richard, *Skywalkers: A History of Indian Ironworkers.* Brantford, Ontario: Woodland Indian Cultural Educational Centre, 1987.

Mohawk Micmac Maliseet and Other Indian Souvenir Art from Victorian Canada. London: Canada House Cultural Centre Gallery, 1985.

Morgan, Lewis H., "Report on the Fabrics, Inventions, Implements and Utensils of the Iroquois, Made to the Regents of the University, Jan. 22, 1851," *Fifth Annual Report of the Regents of the University, on the Condition of the State Cabinet of Natural History and the Historical and Antiquarian Collection,* February 1852.

The Original People: Native Americans in the Champlain Valley. Plattsburgh, N.Y.: Clinton County Historical Association, 1988.

Rose, Richard, *Face to Face: Encounters with Identity.* Rochester, N.Y.: Rochester Museum & Science Center, 1983.

Tewaarathon (Lacrosse): Akwesasne's Story of Our National Game. North American Indian Travelling College, 1978.

Van Horn, Elizabeth H., *Iroquois Silver Brooches (As-ne-as-ga) in the Rochester Museum.* Rochester, N.Y.: Rochester Museum & Science Center, 1971.

INDEX